THE ESSENTIAL
HANDSAW
BOOK

Projects & Techniques for Mastering a Timeless Hand Tool

From the Editors of

CEDAR LANE PRESS

CONTENTS

3   SPECIALTY SAWS

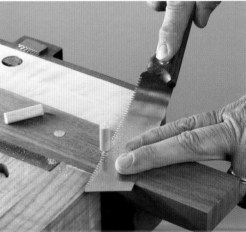

4   ACCESSORIES & PROJECTS

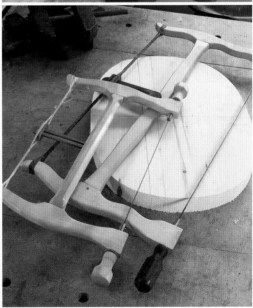

1

BASICS

All about handsaws. A handsaw might be the very first tool most people think of when imagining a decked-out workshop, but too often these humble tools hang on nails, gathering dust. These trusty woodcutting devices have been used for centuries, but have lately fallen out of popularity as more expensive and louder electric-powered saws grab woodworkers' attention. To add to the confusion, terms like "fleam" and "rake" make handsaws even more mysterious to the uninitiated. Let's delve in and learn why every woodworker should take their saw off the wall and put it to use.

THE CASE FOR HANDSAWS

Here's why you should learn to sharpen and use these oft-neglected tools.

BY GRAHAM BLACKBURN

Far from being quaint anachronisms or symbols of outdated and inefficient technology, handsaws are precision instruments that deserve a place in every contemporary workshop.

There are several reasons for such a claim, including safety, convenience, and economy, but of ultimate importance for most woodworkers—whether professionals or hobbyists—is the fact that there are things you can do with handsaws that you can't do any other way. Including handsaws in your tool kit gives you more choices and can produce better woodworking.

The most common and most useful handsaws are a dovetail saw, a backsaw (also known as a tenon saw), a rip saw, and a crosscut saw.

The dovetail saw is your secret weapon for perfect joinery.

The backsaw is an all-purpose saw for safe cuts on small workpieces—no one wants to push a small piece of wood (2" or less) through the table saw without all sorts of jigs and protection.

And crosscut and rip saws can be efficient alternatives to table saws and bandsaws when you don't want to change any of your carefully-set-up jigs, blades, or fences for a single cut. Plus, it's often much easier to take the saw to the wood than vice versa.

Similar to all other tools, any handsaw must be properly tuned and skillfully used to be truly useful. But how

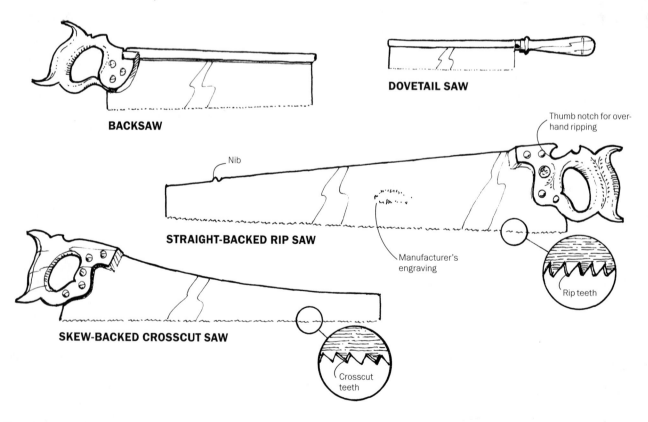

BACKSAW

DOVETAIL SAW

Nib

STRAIGHT-BACKED RIP SAW

Thumb notch for overhand ripping

Manufacturer's engraving

Rip teeth

SKEW-BACKED CROSSCUT SAW

Crosscut teeth

JOINTING

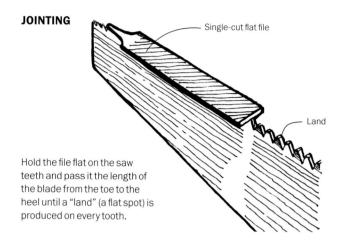

Hold the file flat on the saw teeth and pass it the length of the blade from the toe to the heel until a "land" (a flat spot) is produced on every tooth.

HOW A SAW FILE SHOULD FIT

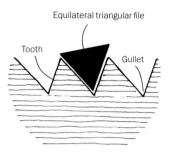

can you tell a good handsaw from a bad one? How do you make sure it's in top condition? And what are the techniques to use it effortlessly and accurately in your shop?

There is very little that is inherently difficult about handsaw use, yet the answers to these questions—for people raised on tools that must be plugged in before anything happens—have become virtual secrets. What was once common knowledge has been largely forgotten.

THE TUNE-UP

The first requirement is a sharp and well-set tool. There are three components to tuning up a handsaw: jointing, filing, and setting. And none of these tasks requires a time-consuming or costly trip to the old guy who sharpens saws on the other side of town.

■ Jointing simply means running a flat file along the top of the saw's teeth. This ensures that all the teeth will be the same height (so they cut evenly) and provides a clear guide for the next step.

■ Filing usually consists of no more than a couple of strokes with a triangular-shaped file placed between every tooth—in a particular manner and order. Three things make this process easy: understanding the particular shape of a given saw's teeth, using the right size file, and using a saw vise or an improvised wooden substitute.

Saws designed to cut along the grain, such as rip saws, dovetail saws, and many backsaws, have teeth formed like a row of little chisels, as shown in the illustration at left. Saws used for cutting across the grain, such as crosscut saws, have teeth filed to look like a series of little knives.

The files used to sharpen Western saws (as opposed to Japanese-style saws) should be equilateral triangular files, because no matter how aggressive the rake of any given saw's teeth may be, the angles formed between the teeth and the angles formed by the teeth themselves are always 60°. The right-sized file is one that is small enough to fit into the gullet between two teeth and large enough to file the entire slope of a tooth.

When you file a saw, you need to clamp the saw in a saw vise (or between two pieces of wood held in a vise) so that the teeth of the tool are just visible above the vise. To position the file correctly, you need to pay attention to

FILING CROSSCUT AND RIP TEETH

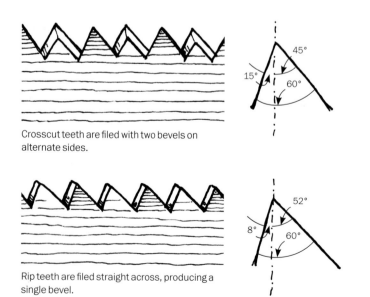

Crosscut teeth are filed with two bevels on alternate sides.

Rip teeth are filed straight across, producing a single bevel.

three things (which are shown in the illustration at right):

First, hold the file perfectly horizontal.

Second, tilt the file so it fits down into the gullet and preserves the particular rake of the tooth. (This angle can be checked by dropping the file into a gullet at the extreme toe or heel of the blade where the teeth are unlikely to have been worn out of their original shape.)

Third, if you are filing a rip saw, hold the file perpendicular to the side of the blade. If you are filing crosscut teeth, angle the file back about 15°.

Now you are ready to file. If you abide by the following rules, you'll never become confused when filing: Always start by clamping the saw so that the handle is to the right, then place the file to the left of the first tooth that is pointing toward you at the toe of the saw. Hold the file as described above and take as many strokes as necessary to remove half the flat spot that was formed on the tip of the tooth when you jointed the saw. Remove the file and place it to the left of the next tooth pointing toward you (this will involve

FILING POSITIONS

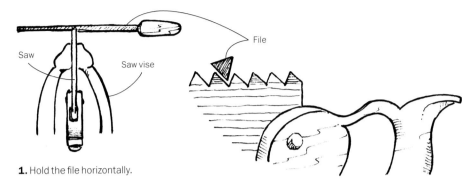

1. Hold the file horizontally.

2. Tilt the file to match the slope of the teeth.

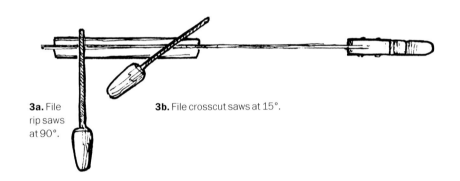

3a. File rip saws at 90°.

3b. File crosscut saws at 15°.

TOOTH SET

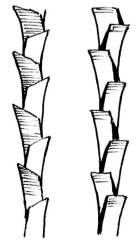

Crosscut teeth   Rip teeth

skipping one gullet) and repeat the process until you reach the handle end. Then turn the saw around so the handle is to the left and place the file to the right of the first tooth pointing toward you at the toe of the saw. File until the remainder of the flat spot is gone from the tip of the tooth, then move the file toward the handle, skipping every other gullet. The whole process should take no more than a couple of minutes.

■ Setting, the last operation, involves bending alternate teeth sideways so they cut a kerf slightly wider than the thickness of the saw blade. With no set, the friction caused by sawing heats up the moisture in the wood, causing the wood to bind on the saw. The wetter or softer the wood, the greater the set needed.

The tool used to bend the teeth, called a sawset, is like a small handheld vise. You place the sawset on a tooth and squeeze the handle; it bends the tooth.

Modern sawsets can be adjusted easily to bend any size tooth correctly. But however great the set, you should bend no more than half the height of the tooth—any more and the tooth may break off. This is not fatal, but like eating, the more teeth you have, the easier the process. Small saws with many teeth, such as dovetail saws, which are used for relatively small cuts in dry wood, need very little set. Large rip saws need considerably more set.

More important than the amount of set is the evenness of the job you do. If the teeth on one side of the saw are set out more than the other, they will cut faster and cause the saw to "lead"—a term used to describe the tendency of the saw to wander from the line you're trying to follow.

Sufficient and even set is therefore almost more important than actual sharpness. For this reason, set the teeth in the same way that you file the teeth: First, set all the teeth that bend to one side, then turn the saw around and set the other teeth. This will tend to even out any differences.

If, after setting, the saw still leads, simply dress down the teeth on the side to which the saw is curving by running a flat file along the side of the teeth. Then check your saw to see if it still leads by making a test cut.

QUALITY TIPS

Even cheap saws can be tuned so they perform well, but quality saws will have more comfortable handles, better balance, and superior blades that will stay sharp longer. Clues to finding a superior saw, old or new, include:

1. Nicely formed wooden handles (the more screws that hold the blade to the handle, the better).

2. A skewed back, rather than a straight back. This indicates a hollow-ground blade, which means the blade is thinner as you move further away from the teeth, thereby necessitating less set and a smaller kerf.

3. Manufacturer's pride, which can be seen in items such as a brass back instead of a steel back on a backsaw, or fancier engraving (sometimes called the "etch") on the face of the blade.

THE BASIC TECHNIQUE

Also essential for efficient handsaw use is learning correct technique. Even the best saw will prove disappointing if you don't understand how it should be used. A lot of this is common sense, but to avoid reinventing the wheel, you need to know the basics.

First, understand that handles are not designed to accommodate your entire hand. The idea is to insert only the lower three fingers of your hand

into any saw with a closed handle; the index finger should be held alongside the handle, pointing forward.

Second, if you hold the saw like this while aligning yourself with the cut so that your eye is directly above the back of the blade, favoring neither side, you will take advantage of your natural ability to recognize verticality. Unless we are sick or drunk, most of us can tell more easily what is straight up and down than we can judge any other angle.

This basic positioning remains true whether you're sawing down an 8'-long oak board or making a 2" cut in a small workpiece held on your benchtop.

Next, you need to know how to start a cut and at what angle the saw teeth should be presented to the work. Whether you're using a small dovetail saw or a full-size, 26"-long rip saw with four teeth per inch, start the kerf by placing the saw on the work near the heel of the blade (the end nearest the handle) and drawing backward for a few strokes. Resist the temptation to push until the kerf has been cut sufficiently deep for the saw not to jump out of it.

KEEPING THE LINE VISIBLE

1. Tilt the workpiece so that the layout lines across the top and down the front side are visible.

2. Then turn the workpiece around so the layout line on the back side is visible—the previous kerfs will guide the saw.

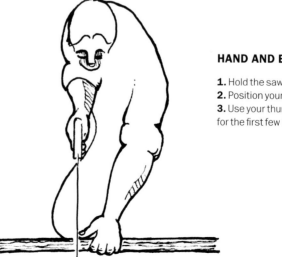

HAND AND EYE POSITION

1. Hold the saw vertically.
2. Position your eye above the blade.
3. Use your thumb to guide the saw for the first few backward strokes.

Guide the saw for these first few backward strokes by holding the work near the blade so that the side of the blade rests against your extended thumb, as shown in the illustration at left. It's very difficult to cut yourself as long as you're pulling the saw backward, but when you start to push forward you must move your thumb.

The initial back cuts and the first few forward cuts should be made with the saw at a fairly low angle to the work, about 20° or so. Once the kerf is well established you'll work faster if you raise the angle. Especially long cuts may require you to insert a wedge or screwdriver into the kerf to prevent it from closing up and binding on the saw if the board has been cut from wood that has grown under compression. When using a dovetail saw or a backsaw, the situation may demand a more horizontal stroke, especially if the workpiece is small and you're using a holding device such as a bench hook.

Remember to use the whole length of the blade instead of short strokes. This is a more efficient use of the entire saw and will demand less effort. In any event, you shouldn't have to push the saw with a great deal of force—if the saw is properly sharpened and set it should be able to cut through the wood under its own weight—if held at a steep-enough angle.

Also, always saw on the waste side of the layout line. This sounds obvious, but it implies that you position yourself and the workpiece so that you can always see the line you're attempting to saw on through the entire cut. It's easy to secure a piece of wood in the vise, align yourself carefully with the cut, then saw past the point where you can see the line.

GUARANTEEING ACCURACY

In addition to the above techniques, remember that in traditional high-end woodworking, the use of hand tools is rarely synonymous with freehand hand-tool use. In the same way that you would be ill-advised to attempt to push something through your table saw without the aid of fences, miter gauges, hold-downs, or sleds, it also is risky to use a handsaw without taking advantage of the shop-made jigs and guides that have been developed over the centuries to guarantee accuracy.

The most useful sawing aid for small workpieces is undoubtedly the bench hook (see illustration at top left of page 12). Easily made in a variety of sizes (sometimes in pairs), the bench hook functions as a third hand for holding a workpiece securely. Also, if the hook is affixed and kerfed accurately, it works as an accurate miter block.

A metal miter box is useful but typically requires an especially large backsaw. You can use a dovetail saw or a regular backsaw with similar accuracy if you make your own wooden miter box, providing it has stops and wedges for complicated angled cuts (see illustration at top right of page 12).

When using either of the above devices, how you position the work determines if you'll get tear out on the workpiece. If you position the work so that the shaped part of the molding faces you as you work, the tear out will be on the backside of the cut and hidden

SAWING ANGLES

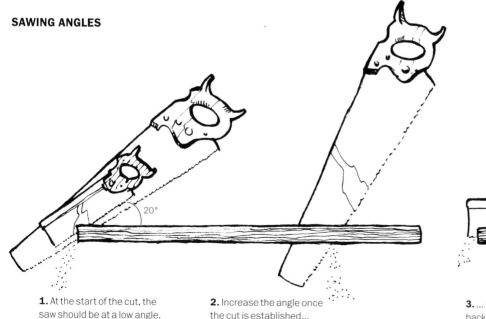

1. At the start of the cut, the saw should be at a low angle.

2. Increase the angle once the cut is established...

3. ... unless you're using a backsaw for joinery cuts.

BENCH HOOK

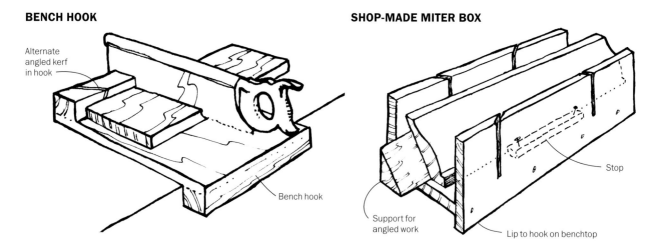

Alternate angled kerf in hook

Bench hook

SHOP-MADE MITER BOX

Stop

Support for angled work

Lip to hook on benchtop

from view. This is called "sawing into the cut."

While bench hooks and miter boxes can quickly become standard equipment in many shops, there are numerous other jigs and guides that can be made easily as the specific need arises. A side guide, for example, can be cut with a face at any angle to provide a foolproof method for you to make wide, angled cuts (see illustration at right center).

One of the easiest mistakes to make when using a handsaw is to saw deeper than intended. This kind of mistake can ruin tenon shoulders, dovetails, housed joints, and many other cuts. Metal miter boxes usually are fitted with depth stops, but there is no reason not to clamp your own depth stop to the side of whatever saw you may be using, thereby guaranteeing a consistent depth of cut (see illustration at right bottom). You will frequently find old saws with a pair of holes bored through the blade—these once held screws that were used to attach a strip of wood that functioned as an adjustable depth stop.

Also, you should take advantage of quickly made auxiliary vise jaws to hold unusually shaped workpieces, such as round or curved sections, and remember whenever possible to position the workpiece so that the cut you make is vertical.

SIDE GUIDE

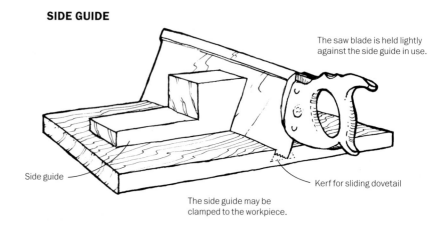

The saw blade is held lightly against the side guide in use.

Side guide

Kerf for sliding dovetail

The side guide may be clamped to the workpiece.

DEPTH STOP

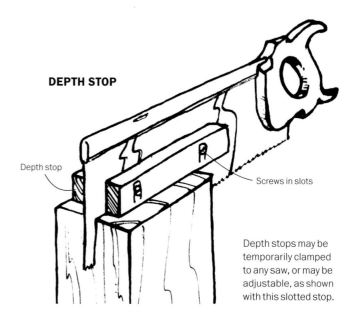

Depth stop

Screws in slots

Depth stops may be temporarily clamped to any saw, or may be adjustable, as shown with this slotted stop.

THE MYSTERY OF SAW TEETH

Pitch, rake, fleam, and set all contribute to the performance of your tool.

BY ADAM CHERUBINI

You may have seen reviews that discuss the attributes of different saws as if their characteristics were mystically endowed by their manufacturers. I'm certain the top-rated saw makers would approve of such a review. In reality, the performance of any saw is based primarily on the shape of its teeth. The following four attributes—pitch, rake, fleam, and set—can tell you a great deal about how a saw will perform. By learning how a saw's teeth make the cut, you'll be able to choose a saw that will perform well for your work. If you sharpen your saws, you'll need to know this information so you can make changes (or avoid making changes) to the performance of your saws.

PITCH: COUNT YOUR TEETH

Pitch is used to describe the size of individual teeth. It is expressed in one of two ways: teeth per inch (tpi)—gully to gully—or points per inch (ppi)—only the points. The pitch of a saw's teeth is chosen in accordance with the thickness and hardness of the stock it's being used to cut. If too fine a pitch is chosen, the teeth will clog and stop cutting before they leave the kerf. This slows the cut. If too coarse a pitch is chosen, you run the risk of splitting the stock.

Over the years, workmen have come up with rules of thumb governing how many teeth your saw should have for a given thickness of stock. I think six

Saw tooth preference. As a community, we simply cannot abdicate the selection of saw teeth to manufacturers who do not and cannot work wood enough to be experts themselves.

Too many teeth. These 10 ppi teeth stopped cutting long before exiting the tenon's 5"-long kerf. This is the reason finer-pitched saws are not universally better.

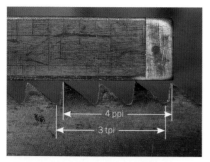

What's the pitch of this saw again? It depends on how you measure it. Either way, this is one coarse saw.

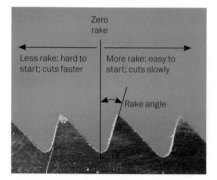

Rake. Lots of folks know the pitch of their saws, but very few know how much rake they have. Rake makes a huge difference in how a saw feels and performs in different stock. When staring down a piece of ebony or lignum vitae, I'm likely to select a saw based more on its rake than pitch.

teeth in the kerf is a good place to start for long handsaws. For example, if you are sawing ¾" stock with your saw held at a 45° angle, then the length of your kerf through the work is actually 1 ¼" long. So to keep six teeth in your 1 ¼"-long kerf at all times, you need a saw that has 5 ppi.

Now if you are sawing dovetails or other joints where the first nick the saw makes must be right on and where you must finish accurately to a line, I think you need to keep 10 teeth or so in your kerf. If you saw dovetails with your saw held perpendicular to the board's face you will need a 14 ppi saw in ¾" stock to keep 10 teeth in the work at all times.

Regardless of what type of sawing you are doing, a saw's pitch is chosen according to the length of the kerf.

RAKE: LEANING FORWARD OR BACK

Rake is the angle the front of the tooth makes with respect to an imaginary line drawn perpendicular to the saw's toothed edge. Forward-swept teeth have negative rake. Teeth swept back have positive rake. A tooth that's perfectly perpendicular to the edge has zero rake. Rake, and not pitch, is chiefly what you are feeling when a saw cuts smoothly or is easy to start. In general, the less rake a saw has, the more aggressively it cuts. Saws with more rake cut more slowly but are easier to start and give you a smooth feel. If you are cutting very hard wood, a bit more rake makes the job more pleasant. But this same saw will cut softer woods more slowly. Choose rake based on the hardness of your stock. If you have trouble starting your cuts, choose a saw with more rake.

FLEAM: THE BEVEL ON THE TOOTH

Fleam is the angle filed on the front of a tooth with respect to the flat side of the saw. Generally speaking, saws with no fleam (that is, they are filed straight across) are called rip saws. Saws with any amount of fleam are typically called "crosscut saws." (Please don't confuse handsaws filed with fleam for work across the grain with the long two-man timber saws that are also called "crosscut saws.")

Any amount of fleam will greatly improve a saw's performance working across the grain. Too little fleam will cause the grain to "log roll," causing tear out. Too much fleam makes saw teeth weak. I think saws with too much fleam cut more slowly.

In addition to fleam, some amount of rake is required for a clean crosscut. You can experiment with different amounts of both. I prefer 20° of rake and 20° of fleam.

PROGRESSIVE FILINGS

A really coarse rip saw is a joy to use, but a pain to start. You can have an aggressive saw that starts every stroke easily without an iron wrist. The teeth can vary in pitch and rake along the length of the blade. This was common before machines cut saw teeth, and, contrary to popular belief, was absolutely deliberate. One saw maker varied the pitch on rip saws such that a 4 tpi rip saw may have as many as 7 to 8 tpi at the toe. It was common to vary rake angles as well. Modern saw filers are experimenting with progressive filings in which only rake varies. You could try varying only pitch. In short, there's no rule that says all a saw's teeth have to be the same. By varying the shape of the teeth along the edge of the saw, you can further optimize the performance of your handsaws.

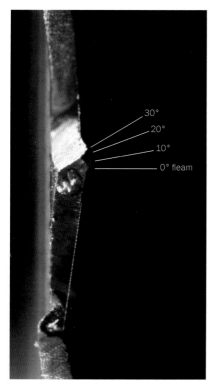

Fleam. Fleam is the angle of the front of the saw's tooth. It helps make a smooth cross-cut—I think. See sidebar at right.

IS FLEAM NECESSARY?

I've read and probably asked the question: At what angle to the grain is fleam necessary? Dovetails, for example, are often cut at 10° to 20° off the grain direction. Should these saws be filed with fleam? I think the answer is "no." I don't think to pick up a crosscut saw until the angle is 45° or higher. But the larger question of whether fleam is necessary is more difficult to answer. Colonial Williamsburg's Anthony Hay Cabinet Shop has no saws with fleam. The scholars there have uncovered no evidence that 18th-century saw makers filed fleam, so they have chosen to work without it. They do however, routinely knife all crosscuts. I have noticed that all of their saws seem to have a bit more rake than their modern counterparts. They also seem to link pitch and rake, i.e. they file more rake on higher-pitched saws. Unfortunately, there aren't many woodworkers relying solely on handsaws for all their cuts. So I think readers should try some experiments of their own. Can you crosscut with a rip saw? How much rake is enough to make this job comfortable? Try it yourself and take notes.

While fleam alone may define a crosscut saw, some contemporary sharpeners add tiny amounts of fleam to rip saws. They report even less than 5° of fleam improves a saw's ability to make an occasional crosscut and may be a welcome addition when ripping hard woods.

SET: HOW MUCH THE TOOTH IS BENT

Set refers to the amount a tooth is bent sideways (perpendicular to the broad face of the saw). Set allows the saw to lay a slit wider than the thickness of its blade. This reduces the friction of the blade in the slit and is supposed to reduce the effort of sawing. What set does not do is allow you to continue sawing when the stock closes up the slit. The solution to that problem is a wedge.

I'm a proponent of set, but not everyone agrees it's necessary. Some say saws

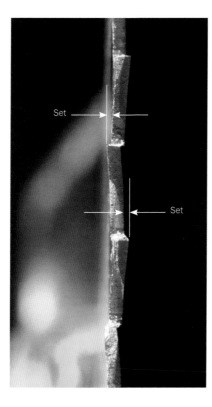

Set. The teeth on this rip saw are moderately set. This blade is .040" thick here. The amount of set appears to be a quarter of that. The amount of set on a lightly set saw is barely perceptible. It may be only a few thousandths ($1/1000$) of an inch on either side. But what may not be obvious to the eye can easily be felt during sawing. Notice how crisp the outer corners of the teeth are. I avoid stoning the sides of my saws' teeth (a common way to reduce a saw's set).

CHOOSING A SAWPLATE

When choosing teeth for a saw, two other factors greatly influence the performance: the length and thickness of the blade (sometimes called the "sawplate").

BLADE THICKNESS

For rough work in thick wood, large teeth are best (small teeth clog in thick stock). Because large teeth require more force to push, a thick blade is better because it will resist buckling. When you have a choice, marry coarse teeth to a thick blade.

For thin, hard wood, you need fine teeth, possibly with a positive rake. This will be a slow-cutting saw if the blade is thick. Choosing a thin-bladed saw for these teeth will improve your speed.

BLADE LENGTH

Your rip saw's blade should be as long as your arm. (You can measure from your armpit to the end of your fist.) Long saws cut fast. But a 24"-long dovetail saw would be nearly impossible to use. Common sense tells us we need shorter saws for precision cuts and cuts in thin material. And that's pretty much what we see manufacturers producing: short saws with fine teeth for thin stock, long saws with coarse teeth for thick stock.

The exception is the 18th-century tenon saw. It was used to saw the wide tenon cheeks on everything from doors to frame-and-panel furniture. These saws typically have fine teeth and thin blades for precision cuts, but are very long, typically 16" to 20". Their length compensates for their fine pitches, allowing quick work through thick stock. Though largely unavailable for the past century, some custom saw makers are now building them again.

So just as we married fine teeth to thin saw blades, we should marry fine teeth (for accurate cuts in thin stock) to shorter blades, with the exception being the traditional tenon saw.

without set lock into the kerf and will stay dead true and straight. My advice is to try a saw without set and see how you like it. I've not found it to be advantageous, but that doesn't mean you won't.

Be gentle setting your saw teeth. Too much force can cause teeth to break and set is easy to add and very difficult to remove.

I think set is especially helpful for work in soft, sappy woods such as pine. Waxing or oiling your saw blade also helps.

There is no magic to handsaws. Remember that pitch is chiefly governed by stock thickness but it can also affect accuracy at the start of a cut. Adding rake makes the cutting smoother but slower. Fleam is added for cross-grain work, and set helps reduce friction. Blade thickness primarily affects the speed of the cut, and the length of a blade for rough cuts should be chosen according to your stroke. For finer work, shorter saws are generally better. Armed with all this in mind, you should be able to look at any saw and know what it would be good for by examining its teeth. Conversely, you now should be able to pick the right saw for the job. Rather than replace a manufacturer's lame tooth recommendations with my lame recommendations, my goal here was to raise your awareness that:

1. There is no standard way to shape a saw tooth for all cutting situations you will face.

2. You can shape saw teeth to achieve different effects (ease of starting, speed, good for softer or harder woods, etc.).

3. Choose the tooth shapes (or the saw) based on your work—not hearsay, my recommendations, or other subjective reviews.

HANG WITH A SAW MAKER

Discover what really matters when choosing a handsaw.

BY ANDREW LUNN

You don't have to be a saw maker to think about saws like one. Some of the most important decisions when making a saw get surprisingly little attention from those who buy them.

Take hang angle, for example—that's the angle formed between a saw's grip and its toothline. I don't think hang angle is discussed as much as it should be or in sufficient depth. Some explanations of it just plain miss the mark. Far more attention is given to how hang angle has evolved historically.

That's interesting, but what about hang angle as it pertains to you right now, making things in your shop? How much do you really know about it? Do you understand it well enough that you could determine a saw's hang angle if you were told to calculate it from scratch?

The truth is, it doesn't take much to make a saw that is functional. The earliest saws were little more than rocks with serrated edges. The real artistry in saws is in their refinement. The ultimate

Choose wisely. While you can get used to most any saw and do good work, select a saw that helps channel your energy properly and you'll do good work more easily.

ANATOMY OF A BACKSAW

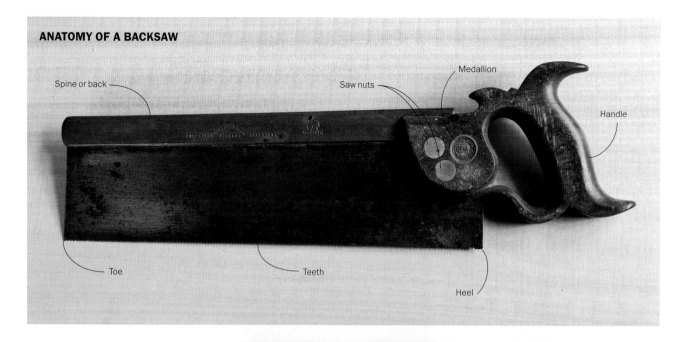

Spine or back

Saw nuts

Medallion

Handle

Toe

Teeth

Heel

test of any saw is not whether or not it functions, but how well it functions.

You can (and should) evaluate that simply by using a saw. But the better you understand saws, the better you will understand what you are experiencing when you use them. You'll know why they feel the way they do.

Let's examine hang angle from the saw maker's perspective.

UNDERSTANDING HANG ANGLE

Simply put, hang angle is the deepest piece of architectural geometry a saw possesses. When you push a saw, the force travels in the direction the grip is facing. That angle has a profound effect on how well a saw cuts. If the grip is angled downward too steeply, the teeth at the toe do not have enough energy behind them, and teeth farther back are pushed down into the wood instead of forward through it. The teeth at the rear will stick or perhaps even jam in the work if the angle is severe enough.

If, on the other hand, the grip is at too shallow an angle, the energy you apply will not be balanced behind the saw's cutting action. Getting the energy

No compensation. A good hang angle allows you to concentrate on your work without the distraction of compensating for your tool.

directly behind the saw's teeth is not the same as putting it behind the saw's cutting action. More on that momentarily. The net effect of a saw with too shallow a hang angle is a saw that feels strangely disconnected from the sawyer and that lacks power.

In either case, the saw does not cut its best by simply pushing the handle

Sweet spot. The correct cutting trajectory is the perfect balance of forward and downward pressure.

High and low. Notice the difference between these two hang angles. The one on the right has a hang angle that is far too shallow; it directs your energy up away from the saw's teeth. I suspect that is why this vintage saw is in such good condition—nobody liked using it.

forward. The sawyer will instinctively apply different types of body English to correct for the poor geometry.

For example, when the grip is angled too shallowly, you'll find you rock your wrist forward with each stroke to create a more aggressive cutting action at the toe. When the grip is pointed downward too steeply, you will find you subtly keep track of the pressure you apply at different points along each stroke in order to keep the saw from jamming.

Even if you don't consciously realize it, your skill and attention are being diverted from the work itself in order to overcome the saw's shortcomings. You could posit a general rule from this: Lack of thought when making a tool results in distraction when using a tool.

To remedy either hang angle problem, the solution is the same. The force applied to the saw must be balanced behind the cutting action of the teeth. What exactly does that mean, though?

A SAW'S CUTTING ACTION

As saw teeth move forward through wood, they also descend through it. The blade moves in both directions at once. You might suppose that the only reason the blade descends through the wood is because wood is removed as the blade is pushed forward—that downward movement is nothing but a by-product of wood removal. But that isn't entirely true.

The teeth do remove wood when pushed forward, yes, but they are not just pushed forward. The saw is pushed at an angle that channels the energy both forward and slightly downward. Downward pressure propels the teeth into the wood more aggressively than if the teeth were pushed only from behind. So the downward movement is in fact part of the cutting action. The cutting action is compound. Balancing the energy supplied to the saw behind the cutting action is a matter of finding

the trajectory that provides just the right mixture of forward and downward pressure.

Every saw has a sweet spot behind which the energy you supply can be balanced—it is applied neither too steeply nor too shallowly. No body English is required. Saws that are the most comfortable and that cut the most effortlessly are precisely the ones that seem to "know" what to do with the force applied to them. All you have to do is push.

Sometimes you will hear people say that a saw should not require any downward pressure to use; that applying downward pressure is required only if the saw is dull; and that the only downward pressure required to use a saw should be provided by the weight of the saw itself.

In fact, all handsaws and backsaws require some measure of downward pressure. Insisting that the weight of the saw be the lone source of downward pressure is arbitrary—if you get it from there, you may as well get it from elsewhere. The weight of the saw is not even the best place from which to get the downward pressure required—the weight presses straight down.

A saw configured to get all its downward pressure from a heavy back feels like you are pushing and steering something from behind to which the handle is not entirely connected.

It isn't about how sharp the teeth are—the sharpest teeth still won't bite as aggressively without some downward pressure. It's like having a razor-sharp carving tool and expecting it to cut without actually being pushed into the wood. Or expecting to push a wooden handplane from behind without getting any weight down over it. A saw can cut under the impetus of its own weight, but that is not even close to the best way to design or use a saw.

It is far more advantageous to account for downward pressure in the hang angle itself—so that simply pushing the handle forward not only pushes the teeth forward, but pushes them forward and slightly down.

FIND THE BALANCE POINT

This is not quite the end of it, though—let's look a little deeper.

If you think for a moment about the finest saws you have ever used, the facility with which they cut is not in fact characterized by a sheer lack of resistance. There is a low-grade resistance present that is perpetually generated and overcome as the saw is in motion. The ease with which the saw overcomes this resistance becomes your perception of how effortless the saw is to use.

The idea is to use hang angle to find the point at which the saw is ever so slightly challenged. This is another way of describing the balancing point we were talking about a moment ago. This

Two very different hang angles. All of the variables in motion make each type of saw something of a separate art.

small amount of resistance gives the saw just the right amount of feedback from the wood. This feedback, in turn, makes the saw feel solid and cohesive.

You can sense the parts of the saw to which your hand is not literally connected. When you can sense the integrity of the tool like this, your thoughts are able to reach through it to the work. The tool feels more responsive.

So hang angle does much more than propel the saw through the wood—it affects everything from how effortless the saw feels to use, to how cohesive it feels, to how responsive it feels. It establishes a direct line of communication from the user through the saw to the work. There is nothing more important than hang angle.

So how do you calculate hang angle? It's geometry, but you don't need any numbers. Prescribed notions about numerical values for it aren't that meaningful. There are too many variables in motion. You are much better off just "calculating" it by feel and by eye. How do you do that? It's easier than it sounds. There's really no substitute for experience and careful observation. Study every saw you come across. Decide what

you think about its geometry and cutting action. With a little practice, you can become very good indeed at sensing how well or poorly a saw will cut.

"Calculating" hang angle for a saw you are designing is really just the reverse of evaluating the hang angle of an existing saw. You simply combine the blade and handle at an angle that you might otherwise admire if you found it on an existing saw.

The really interesting part is that there is no single right answer—the sweet spot is not a pinpoint; it's more of a range. The saw will feel a little different depending on where you land within that range. Relatively small degrees by which a handle is rotated can make a big difference in how a saw functions and feels.

It doesn't take much for a saw to develop its own personality and feel. Imbuing each saw with its own touch of personality is what making saws by hand is all about.

BLADE SHAPE MATTERS

Let's look at a handful of variables that get factored in intuitively when determining hang angle. The orientation of the grip to the blade is only part of the story. The shape of the blade matters too.

The longer the blade, the lower the hang angle must be—meaning the shallower the trajectory needs to be. The energy supplied needs to get behind the cutting action all the way down at the toe of the saw. Otherwise it is like taking a grip made for a shorter saw and trying to push a longer saw with it. The teeth at the toe will cut, but they won't have much leverage behind them. Also, as mentioned earlier, you run the risk of jamming the teeth into the wood farther back along the blade, closer to the handle.

The taller the blade, the steeper the hang angle must be. If the hang angle is too shallow, the force you apply is too high and doesn't get sufficiently behind the teeth—it's like using a handle oriented to an imaginary toothline buried somewhere within the field of the blade. The teeth will cut, of course— saw teeth will cut so long as they are pushed forward; but the force you are applying to the saw won't feel connected to those teeth. Nor will it do a very good job of pushing them forward. The teeth at the toe of the saw will tend to dig in and grab. This is because the force is too high—it's a force that would cause the saw to topple forward if it could, like a bicycle rider about to go over the handlebars.

Some blades are tall enough that it is not possible to get a really good hang angle without lowering the placement of the grip. Grip placement is important for all saws—you just don't notice it as much with saws whose blades aren't tall because the relative vertical compactness of these saws fosters good grip placement in the first place. With tall saws, if the grip is left high, you either wind up with that toppling effect described above, or you wind up with the force being aimed too steeply downward.

Grip placement. Notice how, with these taller and longer blades, the handles have a curious "jog" along their upper edge, so that the upper edge of the blade is supported while the grip is placed lower.

Trying to dial in the hang angle on a saw whose grip is too high is like trying to answer a test question that has no right answer. The solution is to alter the handle design to lower the grip on the handle itself. You see this commonly with handsaw handles.

INCLINED (OR RAKED) BLADES
One last variable warrants attention when discussing hang angle: Not all backsaw blades are rectangular. Some are inclined, or raked, from toe to heel,

Blade rake. This is one reason that numbers don't matter. These saws have the same numerical hang angle, but they won't feel identical in use. The saw with the raked blade is more compact.

Fundamental character. Blade rake is like hang angle—there is no single correct value for it. A saw maker's decisions become a saw's fundamental character. All three of these saws are quite nice, and each is a little different.

so they are taller at the heel than at the toe. Because hang angle is the relation of the grip to the tooth line, you can manipulate hang angle by altering the tooth line as well as the handle. If you leave the handle alone and incline, or rake, the blade, that is the equivalent of having rotated the grip up higher.

Consider two saws on which the hang angles are the same, but one blade is raked while the other is not. On the one hand, they are identical. But on the other, the saw with the raked blade is more compact; its grip sits lower in relation to the saw's weight.

This is important, because a more compact saw will feel more cohesive and responsive.

This is why it's not entirely meaningful to compare only numerical values of hang angle. It matters how the blade is shaped and how the grip is oriented. Hang angle is not just about geometry; it's about how a saw feels.

If a more compact design is preferable, why not dramatically rake all saw blades and rotate the grip down as low as possible? Manipulating the blade is like a lot of things: It is good in moderation. Overdoing it will result in a saw that doesn't feel balanced. A grip too low in relation to the saw's weight will not feel as connected to that weight as a grip left up a little higher.

CONCLUSION

Admittedly, there is a lot more to thinking like a saw maker than I can possibly squeeze into an article of this scope. But I hope this at least gives you food for thought the next time you try a new saw or contemplate one you already own.

Hang angle is immeasurably important. A thoughtful saw maker gives a lot of thought to matters such as this. He or she anticipates the saw in use and designs a saw that reveals its true worth when used. Trust me—the thoughtful maker thinks about the thoughts of the saw user.

But just the same, a thoughtful saw user can gaze back through the saw at the thoughts of the maker. Your experience as a sawyer will deepen for doing so. It would be hard to imagine a better place to start than with hang angle.

IF THE TOOL FITS...

A handsaw and a sawbench sized to the user lead to more efficient and comfortable work.

BY RON HERMAN

One of the first things I do with new employees is fit them to a handsaw. And as a woodworker, fitting tools to yourself is one of the first things you should do, too. Why? If a tool is uncomfortable to use, you won't practice using it—and if you don't practice, you can't master a tool or technique. Instead, you'll look for alternate ways to do the chore. And even if you've already mastered a tool, the easier and more comfortable it is to use, the more precise you'll be. It's like anything else—if it doesn't fit, it doesn't work. Another key to success with sawing is a sawbench sized to fit you.

HANDSAWS

I'm 6'4", and a 28" handsaw is perfect for me—but 28" might be the perfect length for a 5'10" user too, if he or she has very long arms.

The length of a handsaw should be fit to a person's stroke—the length of the arm's push to full extension and retraction—plus the 8" not in use when your hand is against your chest. It does no good to have a saw that is longer than your stroke (unless you're cutting very thick stock). And let's say you're using a sawbench of the right height for you

Well fit. If your tools fit you, you'll be able to work longer, more easily, and more efficiently. Here, I'm showing you should size your sawbench height to be a bit taller than your knee.

Perfectly sized. This picture illustrates the correct length of handsaw for me (it's 28"). Try this with your handsaws—but do it carefully (I'm assuming your saw is sharp!).

A little short. This 26" saw is a little bit too short for me—but 26" saws are much easier to come by in the wild than 28" saws, so sometimes I'm forced to make do—and I can tell you, it's not as efficient.

Comfortable grip. Three fingers should fit comfortably inside the handle, and the horn should wrap around the heel of your palm.

Uncomfortable grip. If the horn digs into your palm, you won't be able to saw comfortably—and you'll try to overcome the pain by changing your grip (to the wrong grip).

(more on that in a minute) but the saw is too long. You could stop your stroke before the plate hits the floor, but it's a lot of work to pay attention to that with every stroke, and you lose the efficiency of your arm motion. Plus, you're pushing (and pulling) unnecessary weight with that unused length of blade. While that little bit of weight might not seem like a big deal, if you have a lot of sawing to do, it will be.

And if your saw is too short for you, the problem is the same in reverse. You can't extend and retract fully with every stroke (and keep the blade in the cut), so you have to use more strokes (and more energy) to get through the cut. Plus, a too-short saw won't pass all the way through the wood to release the dust from the gullets.

So how do you size a handsaw to fit your body? Hold out your dominant arm and place the tip of the blade against your chest with the blade extended down the length of your arm. The sawplate should reach to the first joint in your index finger. Alternatively, use a tape measure.

So now that you have a saw of the right length, are you ready to start cutting? Maybe not. You also have to make sure the handle fits your hand. Grasp the handle properly—that is, with three fingers inside; your index finger should point down the sawplate. You shouldn't have to jam your fingers in, and there should be enough room for your hand to get good blood flow.

If blood flow is restricted, you raise your blood pressure and your heart has to do extra work; that tires you out more quickly. The handle should feel good in your hand, and the horn should wrap just around your palm. If it digs in, you're in for some painful sawing—and to overcome the pain (really, just relocate it), you'll probably adjust your grip and then have trouble sawing well.

THE INDISPENSABLE SAWBENCH

So now you have a saw that's the right length with a comfortable grip. Is it time to start knocking down that stock? Not quite. First, you should build a sawbench.

There are many styles of sawbenches but in my opinion, mine is the best. The height of the bench is even with the bottom of my knees, so when I sit down on it, my feet are flat to the ground and

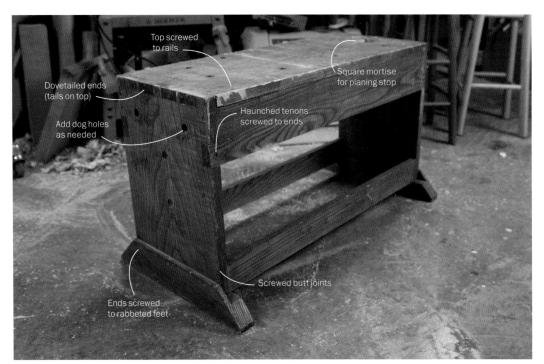

Top screwed to rails

Square mortise for planing stop

Dovetailed ends (tails on top)

Haunched tenons screwed to ends

Add dog holes as needed

Screwed butt joints

Ends screwed to rabbeted feet

A good sawbench— for me. There are various types of sawbenches, but this is the style I always build. No, I'm not going to give you dimensions. You have to build one that fits you, not me.

the top edges don't cut into the back of my thighs. It's the same width as my hip bones, so that I can straddle it comfortably. And it's about 3' long, because that's long enough to be sturdy—and fit in my truck.

See the dog holes in the top and on the sides? I use holdfasts in those to secure a workpiece for chisel work, tenoning—whatever. And if the dog hole is in the wrong location for whatever I'm doing, I bore one where I need it. Notice the open side and bottom stretchers that are lifted just off the ground—that is so I can stick my legs inside the bench and jam my toes under those stretchers to lock my body in place. The way the ends fit into the feet is also important—they're attached in full rabbets with the lip on the outside. I secure boards against that lip when I'm working on the end of a piece, which keeps the piece from damaging, say, a newly laid floor. For the rest of the particulars on how it's built, see the picture above. Now you're ready to comfortably saw.

Toe jam. The lower stretchers are at the perfect height so I can jam my toes underneath to help keep my body in place as I work.

Lip service. With the ends attached in rabbets to the feet, there's a lip at the bottom that I can use to keep workpieces off the floor when I'm working on an end.

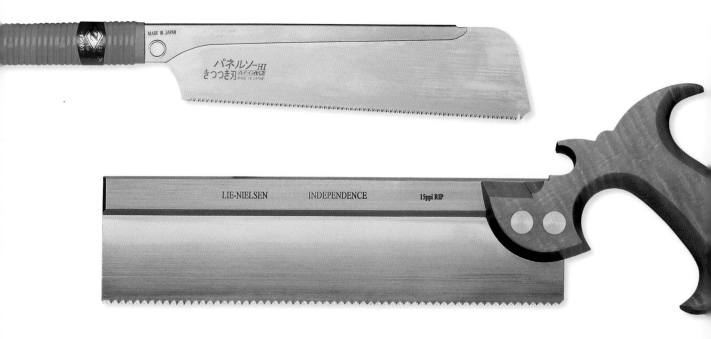

JAPANESE SAWS VS. WESTERN SAWS

The difference is more than just pushing or pulling.

BY CHRISTOPHER SCHWARZ

It might shock you to hear this, but in the last decade or so, more than three centuries of a Western tool-making tradition have been undone.

The Western handsaw, a tool that cuts on the push stroke and was the pride of the English-speaking world, isn't the tool most woodworkers now reach for when they need a handsaw.

It has been replaced by the Japanese saw, which cuts on the pull stroke and once was mocked by Westerners as "backward."

What caused this shift to Japanese saws? While some say it's because sawing on the pull stroke is superior to sawing on the push stroke, the issue actually is more complex.

And which saw is best? The prevailing wisdom says Japanese saws are superior and easier for beginners to learn. But if you've ever worked with a sharp, well-tuned Western saw, you know this can't be entirely true.

To answer these questions, we decided to scrutinize the two types of saws to learn their true differences, beyond the information in catalogs. Armed with this knowledge, you can choose a saw that's right for your woodworking and your budget. Our journey begins in ancient Egypt.

THE FIRST HANDSAWS

Modern woodworkers would almost immediately recognize the first known metal saws, which were excavated in Egypt.

They had long, knife-like blades and straight grips, and they cut on the pull stroke like Japanese saws. Why the pull stroke?

Early Egyptian saws were made with a thin sheet of copper (as thin as 0.03") and had no rigid spine like the modern backsaw.

"(If they had been used) on the push stroke, the saw would have buckled and bent," according to Geoffrey Killen,

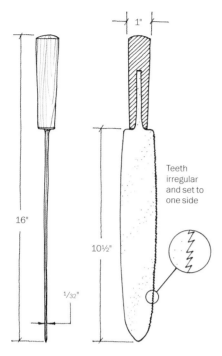

Egyptian handsaw. The first known metal saws hail from Egypt and, like Japanese saws, cut on the pull stroke.

author of numerous books and articles on Egyptian woodworking and the head of faculty at the Design and Technology Department of the Stratton Upper School and Community College in England.

What is unusual about these saws is that all the teeth were set (meaning they were bent) to one side of the blade. This makes the saw difficult to steer, and the Egyptians had to come up with ingenious ways of wedging the saw kerf open during each cut, according to Killen.

The advent of bronze tools brought some refinements, as did the iron saws developed by the Romans. But the basic form was still a pull saw with a thin blade.

It was the invention of the frame saw (plus teeth set to both sides of the blade) that allowed these thin metal blades to be used on either the push stroke or the pull stroke—much like a modern coping saw or bow saw, according to *The History of Woodworking Tools* (G. Bell & Sons) by W.L. Goodman.

The frame saw might not have been invented by the Romans, but they certainly refined it and produced a wide variety of them.

This is an important fork in the road in saw history that affects us to this day. The Japanese developed pull saws like the Egyptians, but they never seem to have developed frame saws, according to several students of Japanese history (though a Chinese frame saw did come into use in 15th-century Japan).

So the Japanese, with their scarce metal resources and their traditions of working low to the ground, stuck with the pull saw and refined it to a high art.

In the West, most of the European continent stuck with the bow saw. But the Dutch and English took a different path. In the mid-17th century, wider steel blades became possible thanks to water-driven mills, and the modern handsaw that cuts on the push stroke was born.

THE WEST STUMBLES

The 19th and early 20th centuries were the golden age of Western handsaws. There were hundreds of saw manufacturers, fierce competition, high-quality tools, and a very hungry market.

But as the demand for quality hand tools declined, so did the number of manufacturers. And quality slipped dramatically.

"Western manufacturers thought it was OK to ship a saw that was poorly set, dull, and had a handle that looked like it was made by a third-grade art student," said Thomas Lie-Nielsen, owner of Lie-Nielsen Toolworks. "You couldn't use the saws right out of the box. It's no wonder the Japanese ate their lunch."

When Western saws suitable for cabinetmaking disappeared off the shelves, the Japanese saws picked up the slack.

"In Japan, the product lines have not been cheapened," said Robin Lee of Lee Valley Tools. "Even products that have been mass produced have not been cheapened."

So while it was tough to find a decent new Western saw at almost any price, the Japanese exported saws that were sharp, straight, perfectly set, and inexpensive. So it's little wonder that the Japanese saw now is in many North American workshops. It was, in many ways, a simple matter of economics.

FACTS ABOUT JAPANESE SAWS

Japanese craftsmen would be quite curious about the way Westerners use their saws. For one, we work on a high bench and clamp our work when sawing. The Japanese furniture maker works on a low sawhorse (6" high or so) and does not generally have a vise.

Western handsaw. Shown here being used by Don McConnell with an overhand rip grip, the Western handsaw cuts on the push stroke.

JAPANESE SAWS

ADVANTAGES:

- The thinner kerf removes less wood, which means less effort.
- The inexpensive saws are of high quality and work very well right out of the box.
- The teeth are generally harder and can go longer between sharpenings. The best Western saws are 52 to 54 on the Rockwell "C" scale. Japanese saws are 51 to 58 for the handmade saws, and 61 and higher for the machine-made impulse-hardened saws. While the harder teeth stay sharp longer, they also are more brittle and prone to break.
- There are many manufacturers who sell a wide variety of saws with different teeth configurations (more than 100 kinds, by Harrelson Stanley's count) for every woodworking task and every type of wood.

DISADVANTAGES:

- It's almost impossible for a woodworker to sharpen a Japanese saw. The teeth are too complex on handmade saws and too hard on the impulse-hardened ones. Handmade saws usually go to Japan for sharpening. Impulse-hardened saws become scrapers or go in the garbage.
- The crosscut teeth are more delicate. If you hit a knot or cut quickly into particularly tough wood, you could lose a tooth or two.
- The saws are easier to ruin. Because the blade is thin, you can bend it on the return stroke if you push too hard and the saw isn't aligned in the kerf.
- Japanese saws pull sawdust toward you, obscuring your line.
- Japanese saws made for dimensioning lumber (not joinery) have shorter blades than full-size Western handsaws. Depending on the saw, the pull saw might require more strokes to do the same work.
- Japanese saws are designed to be used in traditional Japanese fashion on low benches. When used in Western fashion, some Japanese saws are not always as effective as they should be.

Trestles. Instead of benches, Japanese craftsmen use low trestles. Sawing a tenon with a Japanese saw this way is efficient and requires sawing at a less awkward angle than at a high Western bench. However, you need to be in good shape to work this way.

Crosscutting in joinery. The Japanese will use a dozuki (which means "shoulder of a tenon") to crosscut in joinery. There are various ways to grip the saw.

"(Westerners) tend to clamp everything," said Harrelson Stanley of Nano Hone. "The Japanese don't clamp unless they have to. They do some wedging. Mostly they saw in toward a solid object," such as the work, which is secured by their foot, he said.

A second difference is that many Westerners use the crosscut dozuki saw (a saw with a rigid spine) for cutting dovetails, which is primarily a ripping operation.

The Japanese woodworker instead uses a rip-tooth dozuki (which is uncommon in the West) or a rip saw without a back, said Fred Damsen, founder and former owner of Japan Woodworker. That's because the Japanese philosophy on dovetails and tenons is, at times, different than the Western approach.

"When they cut dovetails they don't want the cut too smooth," he says. "They compress the joint before assembly and let it expand and lock the joint."

Westerners want a smoother cut and are willing to sacrifice the speed of a rip tooth. Many Japanese dovetail saws for the Western market have some sort of combination tooth, in some cases a tooth that was designed to cut plywood that also works quite well for dovetails, Damsen said.

TYPES OF JAPANESE SAWS

But one thing Japanese and Western craftsmen share is having to choose what type of Japanese saw to buy: a machine-made saw or a craftsman-made saw. There are important differences:

■ A good-quality machine-made saw is much more affordable than a craftsman-made saw; premium tools cost even more.

■ Generally, craftsman-made saws have softer teeth than the machine-made saws, which are typically impulse-hardened. Impulse hardening is a fast, high-voltage process that hardens only the teeth. While the machine-made saws stay sharp longer, they cannot be resharpened.

Craftsman-made saws can be resharpened and even customized to the way you work. But this is meaningless to Western woodworkers, said Frank Tashiro, former owner of Tashiro Hardware.

"(The sharpener) doesn't know your work; he does the best he can, but it doesn't always work out," says Tashiro, who adds that the best value and performance come from a Japanese saw with replaceable impulse-hardened blades.

However, replaceable blades rankle woodworkers who don't believe in disposable tools.

To counter that, Japanese saw manufacturers say that once your impulse-hardened saw becomes too dull for woodworking, it is still plenty sharp for work in the garden as a pruning saw.

"You can make a nice scraper out of the blade, too," Damsen said of the saws.

■ Another difference is that many craftsman-made saws are more delicate because of their thinner blades. Even the most robust craftsman-made saw should not fall into the hands of a beginning woodworker.

"Just because you have an expensive saw doesn't mean you will saw better," said Stanley. "It's important to practice the technique. Start with impulse-hardened saws. Don't get a pricey saw and break it. As your skills improve you can use thinner saws."

When using Japanese joinery saws, almost everyone agrees that you shouldn't be aggressive or saw at a radical angle. Just a bit of downward pressure on the pull stroke is all it takes, and you shouldn't apply any downward pressure on the return push.

Push instead of pull. Some students of woodworking history think the push stroke was developed in the West because we work on high benches, unlike Japanese craftsmen, who work near the floor on low trestles or beams.

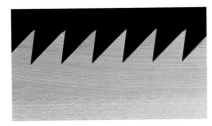

Japanese rip teeth. The length of the rip teeth are graduated on Japanese saws. They start small near the handle and get larger.

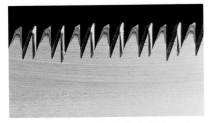

Japanese crosscut teeth. Note the long slender teeth and three bevels filed on each tooth. The tips are discolored from impulse-hardening.

Western rip teeth. Rip teeth work like chisels, levering out the grain. Crosscut teeth work like knives, severing the fibers on either side.

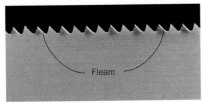

Western crosscut teeth. You can see the simpler secondary bevels (called the "fleam") filed on every other tooth.

FACTS ABOUT WESTERN SAWS

No one can deny that Japanese saws cut very well, but so do Western saws that are sharp and properly set. The problem is finding Western saws suitable for woodworking. There are still some manufacturers of full-size Western saws that do a decent job for woodworking, including Pax and Lynx (Thomas Flinn & Co, Ltd.), and Augusta-Heckenrose. Some of them also make joinery saws—backsaws with a rigid spine on the blade. And companies such as Lie-Nielsen now make premium joinery saws that are the equal of the outstanding saws of the 19th century.

But by far, the biggest sources of quality Western saws are flea markets and auctions. Top-of-the-line Disston, Simonds, and E.C. Atkins saws can be purchased affordably. These, however, can be rusty, dull, and bent. If you have no desire to restore one of these old saws, there is an alternative.

Pete Taran runs the website VintageSaws.com, which is a sawyer's paradise. He takes classic handsaws and backsaws and returns them to their former glory by making them sharp, properly set, and ready to cut. A vintage highly tuned handsaw or backsaw can be purchased there with no fuss.

The site also is a treasure trove of good historical information on saws. One of Taran's primary goals is to teach woodworkers how to sharpen their Western saws, which is easier than you might think.

He sells the files and saw sets you need, plus there is a fantastic tutorial on his website that explains the process from start to finish. And if you just want to get your feet wet, Taran even offers a saw filing kit to get you started. The kit comes with a user-grade saw with freshly cut teeth, a file, a file handle, and complete instructions. When you're done, you'll have some more confidence and a saw that cuts very well.

Sharpening a Western saw is probably one of the biggest stumbling blocks for woodworkers.

"No one knows how to sharpen Western saws," says Graham Blackburn, author of *Traditional Woodworking Handtools* and an instructor at Marc Adams Woodworking School. "I ask the students to bring in their worst plane and their worst saw. Once they sharpen their saws they never go back to Japanese saws."

But if you don't want to learn to sharpen, you still can get a flea-market saw professionally tuned. Taran offers sharpening service too.

WESTERN SAW TIPS

Once sharpened, a Western saw is easier to use than you might think. Here are a few tips:

■ Though it sounds obvious, use a rip saw for rip cuts, such as dovetailing. Some dovetail saws are filed for crosscut. They work OK, but not as well as a rip saw.

■ Let the saw do the work. Don't use a lot of downward pressure on the kerf—this is surely the number-one problem faced by beginners. The saw will wander and you'll never cut straight.

■ Don't clench the handle tightly. Hold the saw with just enough pressure to keep it under control. And use only three fingers—your index finger should point down the blade.

WORST OF BOTH WORLDS?

All this has to make you wonder why someone hasn't built a saw that merges the best qualities of both traditions. Well, a few companies have tried, though nothing has been able to challenge the dominance of the pure Japanese-style saw.

And the reason might be illustrated by the experience of one veteran woodworker.

WESTERN SAWS

ADVANTAGES:

- The teeth are more durable than those on Japanese saws and are highly unlikely to break, even under the worst conditions. The blades themselves are thicker and less likely to buckle in use.
- They will last you a lifetime. The teeth can be resharpened many times. Saws can even be refiled by the user to a different tooth configuration if their needs change.
- With a little practice, you can sharpen a Western saw with inexpensive and easy-to-obtain tools.
- Western dovetail saws that are properly filed for a rip cut will cut more aggressively than the crosscut-filed dozuki that's commonly used for dovetails in the United States.
- They push the sawdust away from your cutline.
- High-quality secondhand Western saws are both plentiful and inexpensive in most parts.

DISADVANTAGES:

- High-quality new or restored Western saws are more expensive than their Japanese counterparts.
- Inexpensive new Western saws are—in general—dull and poorly set compared to similarly priced Japanese saws. Learning to saw with these less-expensive tools frustrates many beginners, swearing them off Western saws.
- While vintage Western saws are plentiful in most parts of the United States, you must first learn to restore them before putting them to work: straightening the blades, fixing the teeth, and sharpening.
- The teeth are softer and require more frequent sharpening, though it is a task you can do yourself after a little education and practice.
- In general, the saws are heavier and have a thicker kerf, so they require more effort to use.

A few years ago, Blackburn was poking around a flea market and discovered a beautiful old backsaw.

The saw had a perfectly shaped handle, but the blade was horribly bent. So Blackburn hung it on his wall.

One day a friend noticed the saw and offered to send it to Japan to see if they could straighten it out. Blackburn agreed. The saw came back a few months later straight as an arrow but with one major and shocking change.

They had filed Japanese-style teeth on the blade. Trying to keep an open mind, Blackburn gave it a try. "It cuts well," he says, "but it feels wrong to me. So it still hangs on the wall."

Chalk it up to this: When it comes to traditional hand-tool skills, it's hard to defy tradition. Now you just have to decide which tradition is best for you.

Sharpening helps. This backsaw cuts incredibly well now that it has been properly sharpened. The handle on vintage Western saws will fit your hand like a glove. Later handles are uncomfortable to use and look crude by comparison.

UNDERSTANDING WESTERN BACKSAWS

Explore the virtues of the once-popular Western backsaw.

BY CHRISTOPHER SCHWARZ

The backsaws that built nearly every piece of antique English and American furniture almost became extinct, thanks to the universal motor and the Japanese obsession with quality.

A basic kit of at least three backsaws—a dovetail, carcase, and tenon saw—were in the toolbox of every English-speaking cabinetmaker and joiner in the 18th, 19th, and early 20th centuries. But after World War II, the manufacturing of these venerable saws went into steep decline with the rise of inexpensive portable routers and saws that were powered by the compact and cheap universal motor.

Handsaw giants such as Disston and Atkins faltered. Their enormous factories were shuttered, and the remnants of these companies began churning out low-quality saws with chunky handles and poorly formed teeth.

But it wasn't portable power tools that delivered the coup de grace to Western handsaws. That occurred at the hands of Japanese saw makers. As Western saws became worse, the high-quality Japanese saw became more attractive to the woodworker who still needed a backsaw or two for joinery.

Thanks to Japan's thriving carpentry trade that still requires handwork (a result of their traditional timber-frame construction), outstanding manufacturing acumen, and a general respect for traditional ways, Japanese saws were inexpensive and worked extremely well.

This was the opposite of the pricey and snaggle-toothed Western saw, which barely cut wood. And so the Japanese saw—which was once the laughingstock in the West as the tool that cut backward—became the best-selling style of saw in North America in less than a generation. And it is, by far, the dominant form today.

TWO GUYS REVIVE A DEAD PATIENT

And if it weren't for two tool collectors, that might have been the final word: Either buy antique Western saws or new Japanese ones. But thanks to Pete Taran and Patrick Leach, the Western saw is today experiencing a revival. The two men had technical backgrounds in engineering and software, but that didn't stop them from becoming saw makers in 1996. They founded Independence Tool and started making a maple-handled dovetail saw based on an early 19th-century example.

The saw, which was made with an incredible amount of handwork,

became a cult classic among woodworkers on the Internet, and the saw began appearing in tool catalogs alongside the pages and pages of Japanese saws.

The Independence saw itself was a technical success. I've inspected and used pristine examples of these saws and can personally attest that they were a revelation when compared to the chunky, lifeless, and dull Western backsaws I used in my first woodworking class.

But the company was short-lived. Leach left Independence Tool and went on to become a full-time tool dealer (his site is SuperTool.com), and Taran announced in 1998 that he wasn't able to do his day job and still make saws at night. It looked like quality Western backsaws were about to disappear off the market again.

But then Taran sold Independence Tool to Lie-Nielsen Toolworks, which was cranking up its production of handplanes but wasn't yet making saws. (Taran isn't entirely out of the saw business. He now sells restored antique saws at VintageSaws.com.) Shortly after the sale, Lie-Nielsen began offering a dovetail saw—branded with both the Independence and Lie-Nielsen names— and then the company began selling other patterns of Western saws.

Recently, other makers have entered the Western saw market. And while these companies are making just a dent in the market share commanded by the Japanese saw makers, it is now possible to purchase an entire kit of quality Western backsaws that work right out of the box. And that is a milestone.

WHY USE WESTERN SAWS?

If you do the math, mass-produced high-quality Japanese saws are a bargain. You can buy a Japanese dovetail saw that works just as well as an expensive Western-style dovetail saw for a fraction of the cost. Plus, the consensus

among many craftsmen and woodworking magazines is that the Japanese saws are easier to start and cut smoother.

So why would anyone (with the exception of a historical re-enactor or pigheaded purist) buy an expensive Western saw? The differences between the two tools are more extensive than the fact that one cuts on the pull stroke and the other cuts on the push. The sawplate on Japanese saws is thinner. Japanese teeth are more complex and longer. And sharpening Japanese teeth yourself can be difficult or impossible, depending on the saw.

As a result of these differences, Japanese saws are easier to kink and ruin, especially in unskilled hands. The teeth can break off in some hard Western-hemisphere woods—I've had particular problems in ring-porous species such as white oak. The expensive Japanese saws need to be sent to a specialist for resharpening (sometimes this specialist is in Japan). The inexpensive saws have impulse-hardened teeth, which makes them last a long time but also makes them impossible to refile. The teeth are as hard as a file, so a saw-sharpening file cannot abrade them. This makes the saws somewhat disposable—though you can cut up the sawplates, discard the super-hard teeth and make some thin scrapers with the steel.

In contrast to Japanese saws, Western saws have robust teeth. When I tally the tooth-decay problems I've had with saws, I've probably lost 20 teeth in Japanese saws but have yet to chip a tooth on a Western saw. You can resharpen Western teeth yourself, or get the job done domestically. Any Western saw can last for generations.

For some woodworkers, the above are compelling reasons to use Western saws. If you are one of those, read on. If you still prefer Japanese saws and want to learn more about using them for joinery, check out the other articles on Japanese saws in this book.

FOUR WESTERN BACKSAWS

The backsaws shown in this article are particular to the English-speaking world for the most part. Traditional European woodworkers still use frame saws, where a thin saw blade is held in tension in a wooden frame, though other saw forms are available and used on the Continent.

Western backsaws are typically separated into four forms, and their details (blade length, number of teeth etc.) are usually traced back to Edward H. Knight's 1876 opus *American Mechanical Dictionary*. But some modern woodworkers are confused about which of these four saws they need in their shop, so here is a discussion of each saw, its details, and the operations at which it excels.

The Dovetail Saw

The most familiar saw to modern eyes, the dovetail saw is the smallest backsaw and has a blade that is 6" to 10" long. The blade's width is between 1½" and 2". It can have a pistol-grip or a straight handle. Most beginners seem to prefer the pistol grip because it whispers to your body when the blade is straight up and down. However, using a straight-handled "gent's saw" isn't difficult. It just takes a little more getting used to.

The teeth of a dovetail saw are quite fine: Between 14 and 18 points per inch (ppi) is typical. However, I've seen dovetail saws with as many as 23 ppi.

Most woodworkers prefer the teeth filed for a rip cut—a rip tooth has its cutting face filed so it is 90° (or nearly so) to the sides of the tooth.

The number of teeth on your dovetail saw should relate to what kind of job you use that saw for. When you have fewer teeth, the saw will cut faster but coarser. The speed comes from the fact that fewer teeth equals deeper "gullets,"

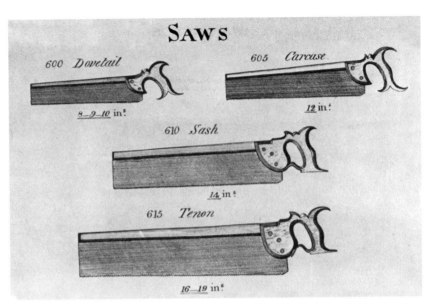

Four backsaws. One of the earliest tool catalogs we have, "Smith's Key," shows the four types of backsaws available in 1816 from makers in Sheffield, England. Note how this tool catalog shows the blades as tapered—they are narrower at the toe than at the heel. There's a likely reason for that.

Two dovetail saws. The saw on the bottom is a typical pistol-grip dovetail saw. Also shown (at top) is a straight-handled dovetail saw known as a gent's saw, so named (we're told) because it was used by gentlemen hobbyist woodworkers in the 19th century.

which is the space between each tooth. When gullets fill up with waste, the saw stops cutting until the sawdust is removed as the tooth exits the work.

So a fine-tooth saw works well for small work in thin material, such as ½"-thick drawer sides. A coarse dovetail saw works better when sawing carcase dovetails in ¾" stock or thicker. You don't have to have two dovetail saws, however. I'd just pick a saw that reflects the work you do most of the time.

Many woodworkers end up using their dovetail saws for other chores, including some crosscutting. You can get away with this many times because the teeth of the saw are so fine. However, your cut will be more ragged than if you used the correct tool: the carcase saw.

The Carcase Saw

By far, the most-used saw in my shop is my carcase saw. This saw is so named because it is useful for many operations in building a furniture carcase. A Western carcase saw always has a pistol grip, though ancient versions might have looked more like a chef's knife with a straight handle and no back.

The blade of a carcase saw is 10" to 14" long and 2" to 3" wide. It typically has 12 to 14 ppi, and the saw teeth are sharpened to make crosscuts. A crosscut tooth looks different than a rip tooth in that its cutting surface is at a 15° to 24° angle to the sides—20° is typical. This

angle is called "fleam" and it allows the tooth to sever the grain like a knife, reducing the raggedness that would be left behind by a rip tooth.

I haven't found the number of teeth in a carcase saw to be as critical as it is with the other forms of saws. A 12-point saw and a 14-point saw cut plenty fast enough for most operations, and they both leave an acceptable surface behind.

The difference I think you should pay attention to is the length of the blade. In general, longer saws tend to saw straighter, so I avoid saws that are 10" long. Getting an 11" saw makes a difference. A 14"-long saw even more so.

Keep in mind that a saw doesn't have to be labeled a carcase saw to be a carcase saw. There is some overlap in the saw forms. Pay attention to the specs of a saw in a catalog or in the store. A saw that is 14" long and filed crosscut with 12 to 14 ppi is a carcase saw, no matter what the tool seller might label it.

Carcase saws are the jack plane of the backsaw family. They get used for everything, from cutting tenon shoulders to trimming through-tenons to notching out corners to cutting miters. I

use them for cutting door rails and stiles to length when working by hand— pretty much any precision crosscut that is on a board that is less than 6" wide. Plus, almost every time I reach for my carcase saw I'm also reaching for my bench hook.

Tenon Saws

When you start wading into tenon saws, it can get confusing. Knight's dictionary says a tenon saw should be 16" to 20" long (that's huge) and 3½" to 4½" wide (also huge). Tenon saws should have about 10 ppi.

Modern tenon saws are not nearly this big.

These ancient giant tenon saws have nearly disappeared, except in vintage tool collections and the occasional modern maker. I purchased one of these old-school tenon saws and was surprised (strike that, amazed) at how easy it was to use, even when cutting tenons that were dwarfed by the saw's blade.

The long blade definitely helps the saw track a line straighter and work quickly—a 1¼" tenon cheek can be sawn down one side in six to seven long strokes. And the extra weight of the saw allowed the tool to supply all the downward force necessary when sawing.

The saw's size does intimidate some woodworkers and they worry that they will tip the tool too much as they begin the cut. However, if you use a second-class sawcut (see "How to Saw" on page 40), then starting the saw isn't much of a challenge.

Some fellow woodworkers have also fronted the theory that this big saw was intended more for cutting the tenons to entryway and passage doors—not for furniture. Perhaps. But I have a couple great old photos that show some real old-timers sawing out huge tenon cheeks. They're using a big 26" rip saw. Wow.

A classic vintage carcase saw. This saw is 14" long and has 12 ppi. The carcase saw is used for almost all joinery crosscuts when building furniture.

HALFBACK SAWS: JACK OF ALL TRADES OR HALF-BAKED IDEA?

Recently some woodworkers (myself included) have become interested in halfback saws, a rare form of saw that was made by several saw makers, including Disston, which made the saw between 1860 until the 1920s, according to Pete Taran.

The halfback was supposed to be a hybrid saw between a full-size handsaw and a backsaw. The small back wouldn't get in the way of many large crosscutting chores, but it would stiffen up the blade enough for joinery.

The saws are fairly rare, so it's safe to assume the idea didn't catch on with consumers. While that would doom the saw in the mind of a pragmatist, I reasoned that the halfback might be a tool whose time had not yet come. Perhaps it's like the low-angle jack plane—that tool was a commercial flop last century when it was invented but is an extremely popular plane in this one.

So I've been using a few versions of halfback saws in my shop for the last few years. And here's my conclusion:

Useful or -less? This custom halfback saw is beautiful, but is it just wall jewelry?

I think the halfback is a good tool for a woodworker who doesn't want to own both a carcase saw and a full-size handsaw that's filed for crosscuts. You can use this one tool for both. It's not perfect for both operations, but it does a yeoman's job.

When crosscutting stock on a sawbench, the halfback is fairly useful until you start trying to crosscut boards wider than 6". Then the little brass back tends to strike the work during the downstroke. When used at the workbench, the halfback is indeed stiff enough for most cuts that a carcase saw would be used for, but it's not as assured a tool as the carcase saw on small bits of work (it is, for example, overkill when crosscutting dowel pins).

So I don't think every shop needs a halfback saw. But mine does. I enjoy using it a great deal, and it keeps me from shuffling as many saws around on my workbench when it's out.

Two ends of the spectrum. These saws are so different in size that it's hard to believe that they both are called tenon saws. The big saw is a much older (and almost extinct) form.

I do have one caution if you choose to get a large tenon saw: The sawplate is more fragile than on other Western backsaws. Historically, the sawplate on a tenon saw is quite thin, and because of this vast acreage of thin metal and the fact that the brass back is so far away from the toothline, there is the danger of the saw bending if it is misused. I'm not saying you need to use your tool gingerly. I just don't know if lending it to your neighbor or teenager is a good idea.

No matter what size tenon saw you choose, the teeth should be filed for a rip cut. Tenon saws are used to cut the cheeks of tenons, which is a rip cut. The carcase saw handles the shoulder cut, which is a crosscut. I also use my tenon saw for other sizable rip cuts, such as when defining the top of a cabriole leg—the square part that attaches to the table's apron. I also use it for laying a kerf down a tenon to accept wedges (a dovetail saw is slow and makes too small a kerf in most cases).

But if you don't think the ancient tenon saw is for you, then you should do what most woodworkers do and buy a true sash saw.

Sash Saws

If you think tenon saws are confusing, you haven't gotten into a discussion on sash saws. Their name suggests that they were used for cutting the joinery for window sashes, yet they show up in tool catalogs and inventories of people who built fine furniture. And there is no consensus among tool scholars as to whether they were filed rip or crosscut or both.

So what is a sash saw? Knight's dictionary says that a sash saw has a blade that's 14" to 16" long and 2½" to 3½" wide. The sash saw has 11 ppi. Those specifications look a lot like what we moderns would call a tenon saw.

To see if I could learn anything about the sash saw by using it, I bought two sash saws that were made to Knight's general specifications, one filed crosscut and the other rip. After a couple years of use I found that the crosscut sash saw was effortlessly doing all the jobs of my carcase saw, and the rip-tooth sash saw had somehow become my daily tenon saw.

This makes sense because the sash saw's specifications overlap with both the carcase and tenon saws, according to Knight's dictionary. What became clear to me in the end is that you might not need a sash saw if you already have a tenon saw and a carcase saw.

YOUR BASIC SAW KIT

I think that most woodworkers who want to use Western handsaws can do all the common operations with three backsaws: a dovetail saw, a large backsaw that's filed crosscut (either a sash or a carcase saw), and a large backsaw that's filed rip (either a sash or a tenon saw). Exactly which saw you need depends on the size of your work and the characteristics of your body. Do you have large hands? Then you should try a tenon saw. Do you build jewelry boxes? Then you should select a fine-tooth dovetail saw.

Once you pick your three saws, I recommend that you stick with that set for a couple years before you get disgruntled and start test-driving other saws. Sawing (like sharpening) is a skill that develops with months and months of practice. And one of the critical parts of learning to saw is getting comfortable with your saws. You need to understand—by instinct—how wide each saw's kerf is, as well as how fast each saw cuts.

Many woodworkers find that certain forms of saws speak to them when they use them. I've let more than 100 students use my saws and find that to be true. Certain people gravitate to certain forms of saws. A few people end up purchasing all the forms. But one thing is certain: After using a sharp well-made Western saw, almost none of them go back to their Japanese saws.

Nice saws, but what are they good for? Sash saws are a bit of a mystery to modern woodworkers. Were they undersized tenon saws or oversized carcase saws? Or both?

2

TECHNIQUES

Learn proper techniques for using and sharpening hand-saws. Nearly every beginning woodworker has experienced the frustration of trying to saw a board by hand and having the blade stick and stutter. With correct form, this aggravation can be replaced with the simple joy of fluid sawing. Read on for tips and tricks to improve your sawing method. Don't forget that a sharp saw is a large part of correct sawing technique—learn the saw-sharpening process here, too.

HOW TO SAW

Practice won't help if you are practicing a poor method.

BY CHRISTOPHER SCHWARZ

Let's begin at the end: dovetails. If you don't cut dovetails by hand, chances are that you aspire to. That's because to the modern woodworker, dovetails are like teeth. A couple rows of tight and tidy dovetails make a good first impression—just like a mouth full of pearly whites. (Similarly, furniture moldings are like our lips. We use these to hide our snaggletooth dovetails and orthodontia.)

And so for many woodworkers, their first handsaw purchase is a dovetail saw. Then they read every magazine article ever written on all the different methods of making the joint. (Well, they attempt to read every article. It's actually impossible to do this in just one lifetime.) And perhaps they take a class in cutting the joint by hand at a local woodworking store.

Despite all this effort, their dovetails still look like a mouthful of gappy teeth from a dental hygienist's darkest nightmare. Why is this joint so difficult? Here's my theory: I think most woodworkers go about learning dovetails all wrong.

I'm not talking about cutting pins first or tails first, I'm talking about tenons first. Or how about cutting straight lines first? Then maybe cutting some slanted lines? Cutting dovetails, you see, is all about learning to

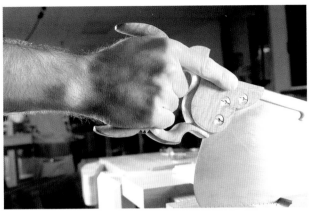

Western grip. On a Western saw, it's always best to extend your index finger out along the handle. Saws are designed for a three-fingered grip.

Japanese grip. On Japanese saws, the advice is mixed. Some people saw with their index finger out. Others extend the thumb.

saw. If you saw correctly, the chiseling part is easy.

The problem is that most woodworkers don't know how to saw. We make sawing harder than it has to be. We hold the saw incorrectly. We work too aggressively. We stand in the wrong place. And we don't know (or don't use) the tricks to make straight and clean handsaw cuts.

Once you master these details, you'll be on your way to cutting dovetails. But you also will have achieved something far more important: freedom. Being able to cut to any line—angled, compound, you name it—is the most liberating experience I know of in the craft. Suddenly, you can escape the tyranny of 90°—the always-right angle encouraged by our machines. Chairs, with their compound angles, won't seem so daunting. Plus, you'll build fewer jigs for your machines.

THE 10 RULES OF SAWING

There's a lot to learn about sawing, from the tools themselves to the techniques for using them. I think the place to begin is to understand how to wield the saw in any cut, whether you are making joints or just breaking down rough stock to get it in your car in the hardware store parking lot. Here are the

10 principles I've compiled from books, other woodworkers, and my own experience.

1. Use a relaxed grip. Clenching the handle will push you off your line. Someone once told me that when you hold your saw, you should pretend you are holding a baby bird and that you are trying to keep it in your hand without crushing it. You want to hold your tool with just enough force to keep it from flopping around and getting away from you. And this is something that you will be reminding yourself of for the rest of your life. It's easy to forget.

2. Extend your index finger out on the handle. A good Western saw handle is designed for a three-finger grip. Mashing your four fingers into it will make sawing difficult and your hand sore. Extending your index finger is good to do with any user-guided tool because it is a reminder to your body to perform that operation in a straight line. Try extending your index finger on your cordless drill, your jigsaw, or your handplane.

That said, this rule is somewhat troubling when it comes to Japanese pull saws. I've seen grip recommendations that violate this rule from people who get tremendous results. In fact, I grip my dozukis with my thumb extended

out along the straight handle of the saw. I suspect that extending a thumb has the same effect as extending an index finger. In fact, early writings on hammers—which have a straight handle similar to that of a dozuki—offer the same advice about extending the thumb for precision nailing. (Yes, there is such a thing.)

3. Always work so your sawing elbow swings free like a steam locomotive. Now we're getting into body position—a critical point. Don't ever work with your arm rubbing your body. And don't move your arm at an angle that's not in line with the back of the saw—your arm and the saw should all be one straight line. This involves positioning your body so all your parts line up with your cut and all your moving parts swing free.

4. Use proper footwork. This rule works in conjunction with the rule above. If you position your feet correctly, chances are your sawing arm will also end up in the right place. Here's the drill: If you are right-handed, stand so your left foot is forward and your right foot is behind you. (Reverse this if you are left-handed.) Your feet should be almost perpendicular to one another, as shown below. I like to place my left toe up against the leg of my workbench because I can then feel how my workbench is behaving when sawing. If my workbench is unstable, then I'll feel it in my left foot.

5. Whenever possible, work so you can see your line. First, position your work so that the line is visible throughout your entire cut. If you are right-handed, this means you should try to have the saw blade cut on the right side of the line whenever possible. (Again, reverse this if you're left-handed.) If you cannot position your saw this way, you need to move your head and peer over the saw blade so you can see the line. Never let the blade of the saw obscure your line. If you cannot see the line, you cannot follow it.

6. Use minimal downward pressure when sawing. Western backsaws have a heavy back for two reasons: One, to stiffen the blade. Two, to give the saw some weight to carry it down into the cut. A sharp and well-tuned saw should require almost no downward pressure during the cut. When teaching the act of sawing, I tell students that their job is to

move the saw forward and back. Gravity takes it down into the cut.

Using excess downward pressure almost always will drive you off your line. It is impossible (for me, at least) to force the saw through the cut with accuracy. Don't worry about the speed of your cut if it seems slow. As your skills pick up your strokes will be faster. Plus, remember this: It takes a lot of effort to correct a cut that has gone awry—rushing a cut will only slow your overall progress.

7. Always imagine the saw is longer than it really is. I picked up this mental trick from a book a long time ago, and it has served me well. This bit of self-deception will fool you into using longer strokes, which will allow you to saw faster and wear your saw's teeth evenly. Most beginners use about half of the teeth in their saw, mostly the teeth in the middle. You should aim to use 80 to 90 percent of the teeth.

8. Whenever possible, advance your cut on two lines. This trick always

increases your accuracy when sawing. There are lots of ways to make this trick work to your advantage. For example, when cutting tenons, I like to start the cut diagonally on a corner. Then I extend the kerf a bit down the edge of the board. Then I use that accurate kerf to guide my sawplate as I extend the kerf along the end grain. I'll work back and forth this way, using the existing kerf to guide my saw.

9. Always work right against a line. This rule is true with all saws, whether they are powered by electricity or by muscles. Try to avoid sawing a certain distance away from a line. It's hard to be consistent. Sawing on a line is always easier. Sometimes you will want to leave the entire line intact and sometimes you will want to split the line, depending on the joint you are cutting. But what's important is that you are on the line at all times.

10. Lifting the saw a tad on the return stroke clears your line of sawdust. This isn't a rule as much as it is a tip

Bad arm position. One of the most common mistakes beginning sawyers will make is they will keep their elbow tucked against their torso when sawing.

Proper arm position. Constant vigilance is required. As you saw, if you feel your elbow touching your torso, you're doing it wrong. Stop and adjust.

The stance. This is what a good sawing stance looks like. All the parts of my body are lined up so my sawing arm swings freely. The rest of my body is positioned in such a way that it encourages me to saw straight. Note how my toe touches the bench.

See the line. If you can see the line you can cut the line. So never let the saw blade get in the way. Sometimes this involves moving the saw (or planning how to hold your work). Sometimes it involves moving your head without violating the rules on proper body stance.

Kerf as a guide. Here, I'm cutting a tenon cheek. I begin with a diagonal cut, then tip the saw to extend the kerf down the edge of the board (left). Then I use that kerf to guide the sawplate to extend the kerf along the end grain (right). Note that I'm peering over the saw's back to watch my lines.

for catching your breath. If you lift up your saw on the return stroke, less sawdust will sprinkle onto your cutline and obscure it. As a result, you don't have to huff and puff your line clear with every stroke (there will always be some huffing, however).

This also relates to the proper rhythm and sound that result from efficient sawing. You can always tell a veteran carpenter from a newbie by listening to them saw. New sawyers drag the tool back through the kerf, making

an unpleasant sound. Plus, they use short strokes because they are using only the teeth in the middle of the saw blade. The old pros make most of their noise on the cutting stroke only. Plus, their strokes are longer. And, as a bonus, they're not out of breath from puffing the line as well.

HOW TO START A SAWCUT

While those 10 rules will help you make a sawcut, they don't help much with the hardest part of sawing: starting a kerf

with your saw. In sawing (as with most things in hand tools) how you begin the cut is critical to how well the rest of the cut proceeds.

If you start correctly, you are much more likely to hit your line all the way down. If you start poorly, you'll spend your first few strokes trying to correct your cut, making your kerf unacceptably wide and fighting the saw the entire way.

There is a good deal of advice on how to begin a cut, some of it conflict-

Use the line. People are timid about sawing, so they saw far away from the line and leave some waste to pare away with a chisel or plane, as shown. Be bold (it's easier, too). Saw right up on the line or split the line.

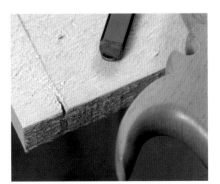

Starting with a handsaw. Unlike with a backsaw, it's good practice to begin with a few strokes that are the reverse of the saw's normal cutting action. The small notch shown is a boon to starting a cut with a large handsaw.

Starting with a backsaw. Nudge the saw to the right by pinching your finger and thumb, which swells them both a bit. Move the saw to the left by relaxing your fingertips a bit and scooting the sawplate against your thumb.

Reflections of improper angles. You can judge if your saw is plumb and square by looking at the work's mirror image in your sawplate. Here you can see a cut that is slightly off square (left) and one that is slightly off plumb (right).

Right on. And here is the sawplate positioned correctly.

ing. One old chestnut is to begin a kerf with a few strokes of the saw that are in reverse of the tool's normal cutting action. That is, if you have a Western saw that cuts on the push stroke, you should begin your kerf by making a few pull strokes. These strokes make a little notch for the saw to ride in.

This is how I was taught to use a full-size handsaw on sawhorses as a boy. The advice shows up frequently in old texts on carpentry, and I think it's good technique when working with the big 26"-long handsaws or rip saws.

However, the older texts are mostly silent on beginning a joinery cut with a backsaw, such as a dovetail, carcase, or tenon saw. So many modern woodworkers have assumed that the same rules for carpentry apply to making furniture cuts.

I'm not so sure they do.

For many years I used this trick with my backsaws, and many times it didn't seem to help much. Yes, it made a notch for the saw to begin in, but the notch wasn't the shape I wanted. This trick made a sizable V-shaped cut, with part of the V chipping across my line and into the part of the work I wanted to keep.

After I abandoned this trick when using my backsaws, my results were more consistent. So here's how I start a

backsaw cut when I'm cutting to a pencil line.

After I draw the line, I place the saw blade on a corner of the work so I can see the line. With my off-hand (which is my left), I pinch the edge next to my cutline and use my thumb to nudge the sawplate left or right until I am exactly where I want to begin.

(A quick aside: Determining exactly where to begin requires you to instinctively know how wide your saw's kerf is. Once you have a gut feeling for that, you will place the tool right where you want it. This is also a good reason not to work with six different dovetail saws with six different-size kerfs—you'll never master them all.)

Now check the position of your sawplate in the reflection of your saw blade (assuming you have a shiny saw). If you are sawing a line that is square and plumb, then the reflection of your board should line up perfectly with the actual board. This trick works no matter where your head or eyeballs are located.

Trust your eyes here. We have an innate ability to sense plumb and square, which is perhaps why we like our houses and furniture made that way (instead of something out of a surrealist painting). If it looks square, it probably is.

This is a good argument for keeping your saws shiny and free of rust—the reflective qualities of the sawplate are an important feature. Also, a shiny saw tends to move more smoothly during a cut, and a rust-free saw will be easier to resharpen—you'll never lose a tooth to a bit of pitting on your saw blade. That's why I wipe down my saws with an oily rag after every use.

Now check your body position and ensure your sawing arm will swing free. Push the saw forward with your fingertips still on the board and against the sawplate (you won't get cut). After two strokes or so like this, you should begin angling the saw to start laying a kerf all along one of your layout lines. Now let all the other rules above kick into full gear as you make your cut.

THE THREE CLASSES OF SAW CUTS

The above advice and techniques are good for fairly accurate work, but not for high-precision sawing—such as cutting the shoulders of tenons. Most beginning sawyers ask too much of themselves and of their tools, sort of like expecting to be able to cut dovetails with a chainsaw.

There are lots of techniques to improve the accuracy and appearance of your saw cuts. But Robert Wearing's book *The Essential Woodworker* (Lost Art Press) organizes all those tricks in an orderly fashion and shows you how to apply them to your work in a way that makes sense.

In his book, Wearing divides all saw cuts into three classes:

■ Third-class saw cuts, where speed is more important than either accuracy or the final appearance of the work. This is a rough cut designed for sizing stock before processing it further.

■ Second-class saw cuts, where accuracy is more important than speed or the final appearance of the work. This is for joinery cuts where the joint will not be visible in the end.

■ First-class saw cuts, where both accuracy and appearance are critical.

Each type of saw cut has a different set of procedures to prepare your work for sawing.

Third-Class Saw Cut

Let's begin with third-class saw cuts for rough work. For me, the interesting thing about the lowly third-class saw-cuts is that the technique is a lot like what modern woodworkers use for all their sawing—so it's no wonder people love their table saws.

The third-class saw cut is fast, rudimentary, and useful when breaking down rough lumber into manageable pieces. I use it only when the board is going to be refined further by shooting the ends with a plane or crosscutting the board to a finished length with a powered saw or finer handsaw.

Begin by marking the cutline on the face and edge of your board with a sharp pencil. I like a carpenter's pencil with a sharp chisel edge on its lead for rough stock, or a mechanical pencil on boards that have been surfaced.

Place the teeth of your saw on the waste side of your line and use your thumb to keep the saw positioned as you make your initial strokes to define

CORRECT A WANDERING CUT

How do you get back on your line when you stray? There are two techniques that I employ. If the correction is needed early in the kerf, I'll twist my wrist for two strokes (and no more) to English the tool back on line.

Most people botch this technique because they twist their wrist for too many strokes so the saw wanders across the line in the other direction. Then they twist their wrist to correct that mistake and they wander back over the line again. After a couple cycles of that foolishness, the kerf looks like it failed a drunk-driving test. If the error is particularly bad, the sawplate can jam in the wobbly kerf.

Remember: Just like working with a bandsaw, handsaws have a bit of delay when steering them. So make a couple strokes with your wrist twisted, then relax to your normal sawing position. Make a couple more strokes and see if you are moving back on line.

Fixing a deep wandering cut. Here I'm laying down the saw into its previously cut kerf to correct a saw cut that is starting to drift across the line. Make a few strokes with the saw in this position and then return to your normal sawing position.

If the error occurs deep in the cut and I've done a good job up to that point, I'll use a different trick: I'll "lay down" the saw. I lower the angle of the saw blade to about 20° so I can put as much of the blade into the good kerf as possible. Then I take a few strokes. The good kerf guides the tool back on line.

the kerf. Advance on the face and edge of your board simultaneously to increase your accuracy. Saw rapidly through the board until you get near the end of the cut, then use lighter and shorter strokes to cut the waste away cleanly.

This is the sort of cut I'll use with a full-size handsaw on my sawbench. Or when cutting wooden pins to rough length before pounding them into a drawbored joint.

Second-Class Saw Cut

A second-class saw cut is used when accuracy is important, such as when sawing the cheeks of a tenon or a lapped dovetail joint inside a case piece. The results of your cut will be buried in the mortise or in the dovetail socket, so appearance isn't of primary importance. But if you wander too much in the cut, your joint won't fit its mate.

Begin a second-class saw cut by marking your cutline with a knife all around your work. You can use a marking knife and a try square—I know some woodworkers use the corner of a chisel to make this mark. When marking tenon cheeks I'll use a cutting gauge,

which is essentially a marking gauge with a knife in place of a pin.

All of these types of marking devices make a line that is almost V-shaped. One edge drops directly down at 90°; the other comes in at an angle—the result of the bevel on the tool.

Now, you can get a little too fussy here, but I try to always put the sloped part of the V on the waste side of my line. This fine point is more important when it comes to first-class saw cuts, but it's a good thing to be thinking about as you make second-class ones as well.

Now, at the corner where you will begin your cut, place a chisel in your knife line with the bevel of the chisel

facing the waste. Press the chisel into the work, remove the chisel, and then come back and pare a triangle of waste that leads up to that corner.

Now place your saw in this notch and begin cutting. The notch ensures you begin the cut correctly. One of the nice things about this notch is that it actually is just like the little notch made with a full-size handsaw when you draw the tool backward for a couple strokes. The cutting begins at the bottom of the V. The difference here is that the V is shaped differently to guide your saw more accurately.

I use a second-class sawcut whenever I'm working on a joint that won't

Third-class cut. This is the most common third-class saw cut in my shop. I'm breaking down rough stock into manageable lengths to work (either by hand or by machine). If I stray from the line, it's OK because the stock will be refined further during construction.

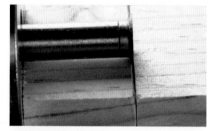

Cutting gauge for second-class cut. You can see how a cutting gauge incises a line that has one flat face and one beveled face. Try to put the sloping part of the V on your waste side.

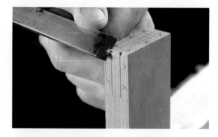

Chisel for second-class cut. You can see the notch I've made with a chisel to begin my second-class cut. The flat side of the notch helps funnel the saw blade into the waste side of the work.

Second-class cut in practice. Tenon cheeks are ideal for a second-class cut. Cheeks must be sawn close to the line without going over. If you saw too wide, you'll have a tenon cheek that requires a lot of work with a shoulder plane, chisel, or rasp. If you saw over the line, you'll have made some pretty firewood.

Chisel for a first-class cut. The chisel is deepening the line made by a marking knife for a first-class saw cut. You might be concerned about the chisel walking backward when you rap it, like what happens when chopping waste from a dovetail. However, the knife line's shape and the shallow depth of the chisel cut keep the line in the same place.

First-class cut wedge. With a first-class saw cut you remove a wedge-shaped piece of waste all along your cutline. The chisel ends up making the critical part of the joint that shows.

see the light of day. Nobody cares if the corners of your tenon are a bit ragged as long as the joint fits tightly.

First-Class Saw Cut

First-class sawing is reserved for parts of the joint that will be visible on the finished piece, such as the shoulder cut on a tenon or half-lap joint. It requires a couple of extra steps, but the results are worth it.

First, mark your cutline with a marking knife on all surfaces that will be cut, just like you did for your second-class saw cut. Then take a wide chisel and place the tool's edge into your knife line with the bevel facing the waste. Rap the handle of the chisel to drive it into the knife line all around the joint. It only takes a couple raps. You don't want to drive too deeply.

Remove the chisel, then pare away a wedge-shaped piece of wood on the waste side, working up to your now-widened knife line. The second chisel cut must be deep enough so that the set of your saw's teeth falls below the surface of your workpiece.

Secure your work to the bench. Place your saw into the chiseled notch and make the cut. By using a chisel to define the kerf of your saw, you eliminate the common problem of the saw's teeth tearing up the surface of your work.

Here's why: You actually used your chisel to cut the part of the joint that will show; the chisel cut created the tenon shoulder. The saw cut began below the surface thanks to the trench you chiseled out. That's how you get crisp shoulder lines with a handsaw—you use a chisel instead.

WHAT ABOUT DOVETAILS?

So which class of cut is the dovetail? That's a tough question. The 18th-century woodworker would argue that the dovetail is probably a third- or second-class saw cut because the resulting joint would be covered in molding. The goal (then, at least) was to remove material quickly with some accuracy.

But many modern woodworkers like to show off their dovetail joinery in a piece of handmade furniture. So the dovetail really encompasses more

aspects of the first-class saw cut. Yet no one I know would ever chisel out the marked lines of every pin and tail.

Instead, we work this joint more like it is a third-class saw cut. What allows us to do this is the dovetail saw, which was developed specifically for this joint. Its teeth are finer than other joinery saws. And the small scale of the saw allows us to get our eyeballs on our work to see what we are doing.

So while I still treat the dovetail like a third-class joint when marking it, I use a first-class tool. (And sometimes, when things get hairy, I'll even use some second-class notches to start a critical cut or two.)

So here we end where we started—still vexed about dovetails and how to cut them correctly and with skill. And while I cannot tell you everything about how to cut dovetails, I can tell you this: If you use the above techniques to saw and practice the three classes of saw cuts, then dovetails will suddenly become much easier.

Sometimes practice counts.

ALMOST-FORGOTTEN HANDSAW TRICKS

Clear your line of sawdust easily, and learn how to mark accurate 90° and 45° lines without a square.

BY CARL BILDERBACK

Dust-free line. Using an orbital sawing stroke, the dust falls away from your line as you cut, much like the wake of a boat. No more stopping to blow your line after every few strokes.

A few decades ago I was using a handsaw in what I considered the usual method: Cut, blow the sawdust off my pencil line, and then cut some more.

The foreman on the job was watching me work and he came over and stopped me. He said he was told many years ago of a way to cut with a handsaw so you didn't have to blow the dust off the line. He didn't show me the method because he said he'd never been able to do it himself, but the basic idea was as follows:

You cut on the down stroke and lift the saw a bit out of the kerf on the up stroke. By developing this slightly orbital stroke, most of the dust falls on the floor.

After practicing this orbital stroke for a while I noticed something else that my foreman had not mentioned. The small amount of dust left on the surface of the work was pulled away from the cutline, like the wake of a boat in water.

This is really neat to see, and I think it is caused by the regular, rhythmic

Push stroke. Here's how to develop the orbital rhythm in your sawing: With Western-style handsaws, the blade cuts the work on the push stroke, as shown in this photo.

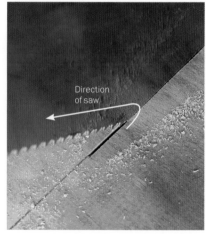

Raised pull stroke. As you pull the saw back, lift the saw up a little (as shown here) so the teeth aren't dragging against your cut. This orbital sawing action sounds different, feels different, and works brilliantly.

You can use the reflection in the sawplate to mark an accurate 90° line across the face of your board. Once you're comfortable with this trick, you'll use a square much less for marking.

vibration within the workpiece that is created by this type of saw stroke. Try it—you will like it!

At one time there was a product available that was designed to blow dust away with a handsaw called "Clear-Line." It was attached to the bottom of the saw handle and directed a puff of air onto the surface of the board with each stroke of the saw.

As a tool collector for the past 35 years, I have looked at thousands of handsaws and have never seen one with a Clear-Line unit attached to it. Could it be that most woodworkers of the time knew how to cut without the need to purchase such a device?

One more neat (and sometimes very useful) trick is to use a saw as a square. This is done by placing the saw in a vertical position across the face of a board. Observe the reflection of the board in the side of the saw blade. When the reflected edge is straight and in line with the edge of the board, the saw blade is set at 90° to the board's edge.

If you want to mark a 45° angle, move the saw until you see a 90° corner formed by the reflection and the edge of the board.

Not straight. Use the reflection of your work to draw a square line across a board. Here you can see how the reflection doesn't line up with the board. The sawplate is not square across the board.

90° angle. When I rotate the saw a bit, the reflection lines up with the board. The saw is square across the width. Now I simply draw a pencil line along the back of the saw and I have my cutline.

45° angle. You also can draw accurate 45° angles this way. When the reflection appears as a perfect 90° (as shown), your saw is at 45°; draw your line.

THE SECRETS TO SAWING FAST

When wielded correctly, the traditional handsaw can size all your stock.

BY ADAM CHERUBINI

Handsaws were used to make some of the finest furniture ever built. They are very clearly capable of producing accurate cuts. Handsaws require little shop space, and produce little appreciable noise or dust.

These facts conspire to allow work in environments or at hours otherwise inhospitable to modern means. Please don't underestimate the advantage of working outside, late at night, in the living room or kitchen, etc. Likewise, the elimination of the table saw—or even the reduction of its use—frees up precious workshop floor space, allowing room for other tools, workbenches, finishing areas, etc.

So it appears in advantage after advantage that handsaws are effective if not superior tools. Clearly only 220-volt speed stands in their way of becoming the one essential tool in every woodworker's shop.

Here, we'll investigate the secret tricks period woodworkers used to saw quickly. Let's begin by examining basic technique.

RIPPING EFFICIENTLY

Ripping at the horse is performed using one or more sawhorses. Boards can be placed across two horses (typically 20" to 24" high), or supported by the broad top of a single horse. Because ripping is defined as sawing along the grain, the cut is started at one end of the board.

Ripping at the horse. Ripping with a sawhorse is surprisingly fast and effective. Here (dressed in the traditional garb I wear at Pennsbury Manor), I'm using the more heavily raked teeth at the toe of the saw to help start the cut.

HANDSAW ANATOMY

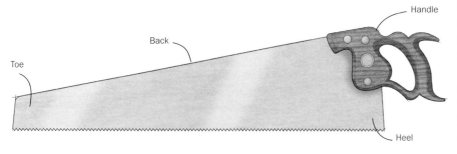

The cut is started with the finer, heavily raked teeth at the toe of the rip saw. Using the knuckle of your thumb or forefinger to steady the blade, draw the saw backward to create a small nick. Use very light strokes for the first cuts. Don't allow the full weight of the saw to rest against the board. These first motions can be very short, using just the fine teeth at the toe.

Once the saw starts cutting, full strokes can be used. The saw should be held more vertical than horizontal, say 45° to 60° with respect to the board's face. Don't force the saw into the cut as if it's a knife. Let the saw's weight provide the force for the cut. Relax your grip. Focus on placing your effort behind the teeth. These strokes are performed with the arm only. The

shoulders must remain fixed, as twisting moves the hand sideways. The hand should move from armpit to full extension, in a nice straight line. In time, this motion will become second nature.

To correct a wayward cut, lower the angle the saw makes with the board. The saw will now ride in a much longer kerf. Push the heel of the saw sideways, ever so slightly back to the line with each passing stroke. The effort of sawing will likely be increased as the blade is forced into a curved shape. If the effort becomes too great or the mis-cut too severe, return the saw to the previously straighter section and lay it down. Lay a new kerf through the mis-cut area. See the photo at right for more details.

If the cut is not perpendicular through the thickness, there's no way to fix it during the saw cut. Resist the

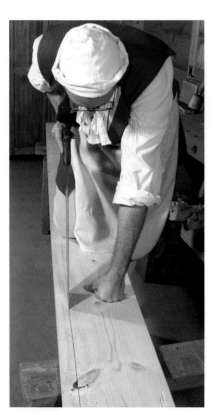

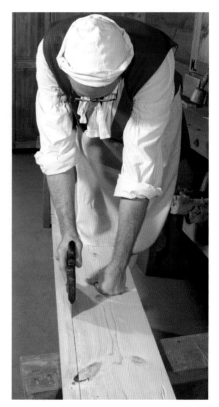

Continue the rip cut. Try to limit the amount of motion in your upper body when ripping or crosscutting.

temptation to twist the saw or bend it sideways to correct. This won't help. This must be fixed later with a hand plane, but then nearly all long rip saw cuts must be cleaned up regardless of the tool that does the ripping. Next time, leave a little extra room to the line. Leaving a little extra beyond the line is no great sin in rip sawing. The planing goes so quickly, one can't honestly say it's a waste of time, only a waste of wood.

CROSSCUTTING WIDE BOARDS AND PANELS

Because crosscuts are often related to the long edge (often perpendicular) they are typically performed after ripping and edge planing is finished. The resulting cut is often the finish cut (not like a rough cut with a rip). Moreover, planing end grain is difficult. For these reasons, extra care should be taken to produce a straight and square crosscut.

Depending on the length of the resulting scrap or offcut, crosscutting is performed either using the bench hook or a pair of sawhorses. The line to be cut should be carefully knifed across the face of the board. A square mark is then knifed through the thickness with the try square. Make this mark on the far edge of the board (where the cut is about to begin).

Drawing the saw back slowly at a 45° angle to the work, nick the far corner. Begin the saw cut with light, careful strokes. Advance on both lines (across the face and through the thickness) simultaneously. This is a critical skill worth practicing, as it will be later used for all crosscuts and many joinery operations, including dovetailing. When the cut through the thickness is complete, lay the saw down and advance the cut only on the face line, using the existing kerf to guide the saw. Maintain

this relatively low angle (maybe 30°) until a sizable kerf is created. With a good-sized slit to guide your saw, begin incrementally raising the angle as you saw through the stock. Your saw should make a 45° angle when you reach the end of the cut. As always, make sure the scrap is well supported before finishing the cut.

PICKING UP SPEED

I find a sharp saw cuts faster than a dull one (not hard to believe). Sharpening a saw isn't as difficult as honing a plane iron, though it takes about the same amount of time to learn and perform. Selecting the right saw for the job (see "Good Saws" on page 55) is a major contributor to sawing speed. In general, saws with lower rakes cut faster. Even faster than a low rake is a saw with no rake or negative rake (forward-swept teeth). Handles that focus all effort behind the teeth seem more efficient to me and thus make sawing faster. Of course, these benefits come at some price. But generally, learning more about how saw teeth work, and optimizing your saws for your work, is an important first step to learning to saw faster.

In addition to a good saw, good technique makes a significant contribution to speed. With proper technique and practice, you'll be able to rip 4'-long 4/4 stock in a few minutes. The ripped edge will need to be planed to achieve a straight, square edge, but that process goes quickly and would be performed regardless of the voltage of the saw used. But good saws and technique can take you only so far. There is a limit to the speed achievable. I believe that limit is still far below the reasonable expectations of modern craftsmen.

Before we reject our handsaws it may be helpful to look back in history to see what we might learn from 18th-century craftsmen.

Eighteenth-century account books indicate craftsmen sometimes purchased lumber in "scantlen." This may provide some explanation for pre-industrial woodworkers' productivity. Scantlen was a term used to describe boards purchased at some desired dimensions straight from the mill. Craftsmen could purchase stock in the sizes they needed to limit the amount of sawing required in-house. Mills at the time, not unlike modern lumberyards, had specialized machinery and personnel that could dimension lumber faster than individual shops. Some 18th-century mills in Philadelphia advertised that they had lumber sized

for certain industries in stock and ready for immediate delivery. Surely this was done in response to a demand from area craftsmen who found such a service cost-effective.

Modern period woodworkers rely heavily on project plans made from extant pieces. Unfortunately the original builders' plans are lost. It could be that the plans were drawn on scrap wood that later fueled the shop's heating system. Or perhaps we have failed to recognize their plans simply because their plans don't look like plans we use today. Artists generally don't care if their canvas is 12" tall or 200". Beauty isn't contained in these numbers. The proportions are what we see, not inches. Period craftsmen may have worked parametrically, using existing stock to define key dimensions. In this way,

GOOD GRIPS

One hand. All handsaws are held in a similar manner. Three fingers and the thumb grip the handle lightly. The index finger points, laying along the side of the handle or blade.

Two hands. Most rip saws with closed or ring-type handles have room for four fingers. These handles allow a two-handed grip. You can pass the thumb of the off hand through the space not used by your dominant hand's forefinger. The other fingers wrap over the top. You will likely find the handle has been designed to permit this grip.

Overhand grip. While this looks uncomfortable, it is highly effective. I find it is especially helpful when sawing thick stock, as it limits the number of teeth in the kerf and keeps the kerf free of tooth-clogging sawdust.

they could use their materials more efficiently, limit the labor required, and work directly to the desires of their customers.

Now you know a secret I've spent years learning. If you don't understand this mystery, unplug your table saw and start relying on your handsaw. After you've learned to sharpen and use it correctly, you too will find clever ways to keep it hanging from the nail in the wall. No saw can cut as fast as that.

GOOD SAWS

Choosing the right saw for the job at hand is an important hurdle.

RIP SAW

A good rip saw blade should be as long as your arm. For work with 4/4 to 8/4 softwoods, I recommend a coarsely toothed saw. Teeth should vary from 5 teeth per inch (tpi) at the heel to 7 to 8 tpi at the toe. Similarly, the rake angle should vary from nearly 0° at the heel to 20° or even 30° at the toe. A "salmon belly" is an advantage, though I'm not sure I understand exactly why. This type of saw—sometimes also referred to as a "breasted" saw—is when the blade is a bit convex at the toothline. For ripping hard wood, the saw can be finer pitched. You want 6 to 8 tpi at the heel in a good hardwood ripper. If you can have only one, always choose the finer-toothed saw.

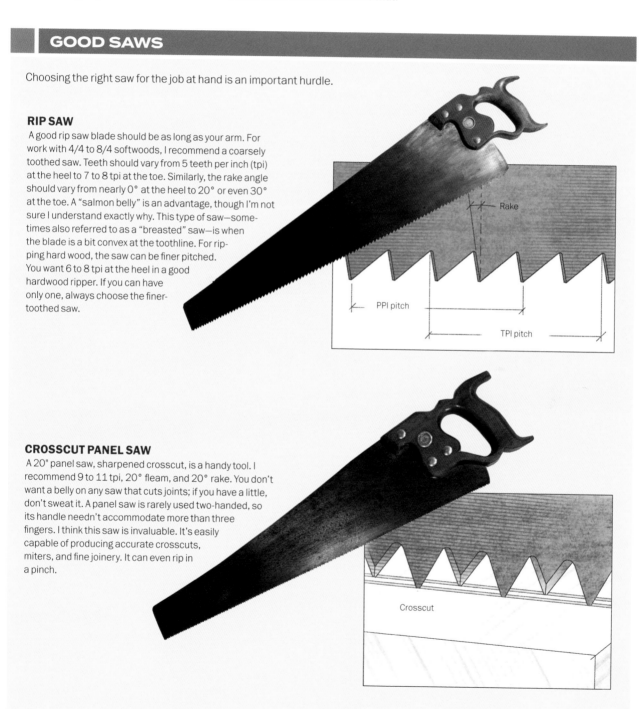

CROSSCUT PANEL SAW

A 20" panel saw, sharpened crosscut, is a handy tool. I recommend 9 to 11 tpi, 20° fleam, and 20° rake. You don't want a belly on any saw that cuts joints; if you have a little, don't sweat it. A panel saw is rarely used two-handed, so its handle needn't accommodate more than three fingers. I think this saw is invaluable. It's easily capable of producing accurate crosscuts, miters, and fine joinery. It can even rip in a pinch.

YOUR FIRST HANDCUT DOVETAILS

The right techniques and tools (plus a few tricks) will give you a good start on mastering this fine traditional joint.

BY LONNIE BIRD

Dovetails have long been recognized as the premier joint for casework and drawers—and for good reason. They're the strongest way to join the corners of a box, and they look great.

However, dovetails also have a reputation as a difficult joint to master. But cutting dovetails by hand only looks difficult. It's actually just a process of sawing and chiseling to a line. It's that easy. (And with a bit of practice, everyone can saw and chisel to a line.) In fact, when I teach dovetailing, I start people out not by cutting dovetails, but just sawing to a line. Once you've mastered sawing to a line, you're on your way to creating this time-honored joint.

No doubt you've seen the multitude of jigs available for routing dovetails. But there are several good reasons for skipping the jigs and learning to cut dovetails with hand tools. Undoubtedly the main reason is the pleasure that comes when crafting the joint with a saw, chisel, and mallet. Cutting dovetails is fun. Another reason is the personal satisfaction of meeting the challenge head-on. And once you develop the skills, you'll find that you can cut a variety of dovetail joints that can't be produced with a jig. Keep reading, and I'll show you step by step how to lay out and cut woodworking's most beautiful joint.

A FEW TERMS

Before diving in, it's helpful to understand some of the terms associated with dovetails. All dovetails have two mating parts: tails and pins. Tails are usually wider than pins and are tapered on the face. Pins are narrow and tapered on the ends. It's the tapered, mechanical interlock, combined with the long-grain gluing surfaces, that give dovetail joints their tremendous strength.

Through-dovetails are the most common type; the joint is aptly named because each member of the joint goes "through" the adjacent member. Consequently, through-dovetails can be viewed from either face.

Half-blind dovetails can only be viewed from one face; on the adjacent face the joint is hidden. On a typical drawer, through-dovetails are used to join the side pieces to the back and half-blind dovetails join the sides to the drawer front.

All dovetails have baselines; the baseline indicates the height of the tail or pin.

TOOLS

The tools for dovetailing are not expensive but it's important to have the right ones. It's also important to have them well-tuned.

Before cutting a dovetail you'll need to do a bit of measuring and marking,

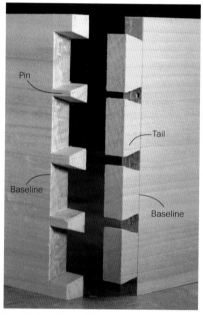

Dovetail anatomy. The essential parts of a through-dovetail joint.

commonly referred to as layout. Good layout is essential. Remember: Dovetailing is the simple act of sawing and chiseling to a line; if the line is inaccurate, the joint won't fit together.

One of the most important tasks is marking baselines. The baseline is created with a marking gauge—a simple tool that consists of a head, beam, and cutter. The head slides along the beam and locks in place with a thumbscrew. Some gauges use a steel pin for the cutter while others use a tiny wheel.

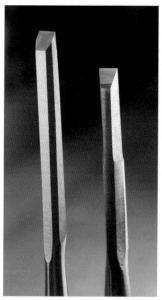

Lonnie Bird's essential toolkit for dovetailing. (From top): A mallet, a marking gauge, chisel (note the shortened handle), an adjustable square, a dovetail saw, a dovetail marker, more chisels, and a knife.

(far right)
Too square. Many modern chisels have sides that are too square for getting into the triangular sockets between the joint's tails (left). I recommend grinding the sides down almost to the back (right).

Either type of cutter will work so long as it's sharp. A dull marking gauge will tear the fibers, making it difficult or impossible to craft a clean dovetail joint. In contrast, a sharp gauge will cleanly sever the tough end-grain fibers to create an incised layout line. As you chisel out the waste between the tails and pins, the edge of the chisel will drop precisely into the baseline to give you that great fit that you're striving for.

Other layout tools you'll need include a layout knife, a square, and a dovetail marker. A craft knife works well; it's razor sharp and the narrow point will easily scribe between the tails and pins. The type of square is unimportant as long as it is 90°; I prefer combination squares for their precision and versatility. To mark the angle of the tails and pins, I use a dovetail marker. One with a simple extruded aluminum design is best; they are inexpensive and I can rework the soft aluminum to an angle of my choosing, typically 14°. A 14° pitch provides the good looks and mechanical interlock that I'm always after.

Of course, you'll also need a dovetail saw, a few chisels, and a mallet. There are two types of dovetail saws avail-

able today: Western style and Japanese. Traditional Western-style dovetail saws cut on the push stroke and feature a thick back to stiffen the blade and prevent it from buckling. However, Japanese saws cut on the pull stroke, which places the blade in tension during the cut so it doesn't have the tendency to buckle. Consequently, Japanese saws have a thinner blade and cut a finer kerf. Also, the unique tooth design of the Japanese saws cause them to cut

more aggressively than Western saws. Which is best? When I teach dovetailing I encourage people to experiment with each. Although most choose the Japanese saws, others feel they get more control and a truer cut with the Western saw. Regardless of which style that you prefer, it's important to use a high-quality dovetailing saw.

The best chisel for chopping waste from between the tail and pins is a short one. A short chisel provides the control

Mark the baseline. Do so on the faces of both the pin board and the tail board with a marking gauge. Also mark the baseline on the long edges of the tail board.

Mark the pin shapes. Use your dovetail square to mark the shape of the pins on the end grain. Then mark the face of the pins using your adjustable square.

you need when driving the chisel with a mallet; long chisels are designed for paring. For many years I've used the long-discontinued Stanley #750 socket chisels. The short 9" length and perfect balance of these old tools are just what's needed for dovetailing. Stanley #750s are still available from old tool dealers, and Lie-Nielsen Toolworks has begun manufacturing its own improved version of these venerable chisels. Of course, if you already own a set of inexpensive chisels, you can also do what many of my students do—cut the excess length from the handle. Although it may sound odd, reducing the handle length greatly improves the balance of a long, top-heavy chisel. And the improvement will be reflected in the quality of your dovetails.

An important step to fine-tune chisels for dovetailing is to further bevel the sides of the blade up by the cutting edge. On most new chisels, the sides are too square, and the excess steel crushes the fibers of the tails and pins as you chisel the waste. Grinding the sides close to a knife-edge will eliminate the problem. Of course, you should also hone the chisels to razor sharpness.

Having the right mallet is important, too. I've found that a round, 12-ounce mallet works best. Heavier mallets are tiring to use and the extra weight just isn't needed. Also, the head of a square mallet must always be aligned to the chisel before striking. Not so with a round mallet.

Once you've gathered your tools and tuned them up, you're ready to begin.

LAYOUT

The first step in the layout process is to mark the baselines. Note that the baseline is marked on both faces of both halves of the joint. It's also necessary to mark the baseline on the edges of the tail board. First, set the gauge to the thickness of the stock. As you mark the

Start the saw. Use your thumb as a guide to start the kerf of your saw in the edge closest to you. After a couple strokes, begin to lower the angle of the blade.

Extra kerfs. To make the waste between your pins easier to remove, cut several extra kerfs in the waste. Take care not to cross the baseline of the joint.

baseline, focus on keeping the head of the marking gauge firmly against the end of the stock. To avoid tearing the grain, make several light passes with the gauge as opposed to one heavy cut.

Mark the half pins on each corner of the pin board, and then divide the board into the number of desired tails. Each point of the divider becomes the center of a pin. After marking the slope of the pins on the end of the stock, mark the face with a square.

SAWING

As I stated earlier, dovetailing is essentially sawing and chiseling to a line. Once you've mastered that technique you can cut great-looking dovetails.

Start by positioning the saw on the near corner of the stock and pull the saw to establish a small kerf. During this initial cut, it's helpful to use your thumb to guide the saw. As you pull the saw toward you, lower the blade into the stock to establish the top line.

Now use long, smooth strokes to follow the line on the face of the stock. Stop when you've reached the baseline. Once you've sawn all the pins, make several extra saw kerfs into the waste area between the pins. These cuts will

make it a lot easier to chisel the waste between the pins.

Next, select a narrow chisel, ⅜" or ½", and make certain that it is razor sharp. A narrow chisel has less cutting resistance than a wider chisel and you'll have better control of the tool.

To remove the waste between the pins, it's best to cut halfway through the stock from each face. But remove the bulk of the wood first by positioning the chisel about ¹⁄₁₆" away from the baseline. Drive the chisel halfway through the stock, flip the stock over, and repeat (see sequence photos on page 60).

Position the edge of the chisel in the baseline (note how easily it drops into the incised line) and repeat the process. It's good practice to undercut the baseline very slightly. The undercut surface ensures a tight fit and doesn't weaken the joint. (Remember that the strength comes from the interlocking tails and pins as well as the long-grain gluing surfaces.)

Now examine the end-grain surface very closely. You should see a fine line along the edge of the stock that was created by the marking gauge. If you don't see this line, you've chiseled too far—or not far enough.

LAY OUT THE TAILS

The tail board layout is created from the pin board. First, position the tail board face down on the bench. Next, place the pin board over the tail board, align the face with the baseline of the tail board, and then clamp it in place. Remember, too, that the wide part of each pin should be facing the inside of the joint.

Mark the tails with your layout knife. Position the blade of the knife against the pin and then use the pin to guide the cut. To complete the layout, mark the end of each tail with a knife and square.

Sawing the tails is similar to sawing the pins, except you'll have to tilt the blade on the vertical axis. I think it's bad practice to angle the tail board in the vise; it's best to learn to angle the saw instead. Otherwise, when sawing the tails of a wide board for large casework, one corner of the board will be positioned high up in the air which will make sawing difficult. Instead, clamp the tail board in the vise (make sure it's level) and saw all the cuts one direction. Then, saw all the cuts that are angled the opposite direction.

I use the same technique for chiseling the waste as I use on the pins; make a few extra saw kerfs and chisel halfway from each face. Remember to undercut this end-grain surface slightly. However, be careful to not undercut the surfaces at each corner. Otherwise, you'll see a distracting void in the assembled joint.

REMOVE WASTE AND ASSEMBLE

1. Removing waste between the pins. First, position the chisel $1/16"$ from the baseline and cut halfway through the thickness of the board.

2. Flip. Flip the board over and do the same on the opposite side.

3. Angle the chisel. To chisel out the rest of the waste, place your chisel into the baseline and undercut the joint just a bit by angling the chisel as shown.

4. Halfway on each side. Cut halfway through the waste on one side. Flip the board over and repeat.

5. Baseline remains. Here you can see what's left of the baseline after removing the waste. This fine line is the evidence that you've chiseled to the correct point.

To assemble the joint, first position the pin board upright in the vise. Now gently press the tail board into the pin board using pressure from your thumbs. When assembling dovetails on wide casework, I'll use gentle taps from a dead-blow mallet. You can hear and feel where a portion of the joint may be too tight. Simply pare a shaving from any such areas, slide the joint together, and step back and admire your work. With patience, you'll find that dovetailing is one of woodworking's most pleasurable tasks.

6. Mark tails. Clamp your pin board to the mating tail board and transfer the shape of the joint to the tail board using your marking knife.

7. Clamp it up. Clamp your tail board vertically in your vise and saw the shape of the tails. Make a few extra kerfs in the waste and chisel it out much like you did with the pins.

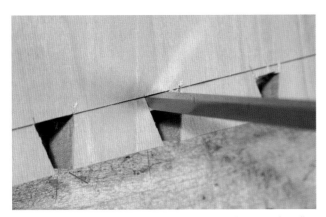

8. Complete chiseling. When you remove the waste between the tails, slightly undercut the end grain between the tails—except on the ends, where it will show.

9. Assemble. In wide casework especially, you may need a few taps of a dead-blow mallet.

SOUP UP YOUR SAWING SAVVY

Good practice makes perfect—or at least better.

BY BOB ROZAIESKI

Hand-tool workhorses. In my shop, my handsaws are in constant use. But even if you do all your rough cutting with the help of electricity, you may benefit from a little practice with a long saw.

When it comes to using hand tools, good technique is everything. We can spend hours sawing, chopping, and planing, but if we don't practice good technique, all we are doing is getting good at bad habits. To really become proficient with our hand tools, the secret isn't more practice; it's practicing better technique.

Nowhere is this more true than when using a handsaw. So often, the struggles that we have making accurate crosscuts and rips, and sawing joinery,

can be attributed to difficulty tracking a straight line. So we buy better saws and practice more, hoping to cut that perfect dovetail. But often, the improvement is only marginal.

It can be frustrating when your skills seem to hit a plateau. But it may not be your fault. You may simply be practicing old, bad habits. Just like anything else, sawing by hand takes practice. But to do it well, it takes proper practice of good technique.

EQUIP YOURSELF PROPERLY

While proper practice is the most important aspect of learning to be a good sawyer, we can't overlook our equipment. It's true that a good sawyer can track a line with a butter knife. But a well-set-up saw, and a proper bench to use it on, will make learning to be a good sawyer much less frustrating.

Most important, your saw needs to be sharp. Also, look at the tooth line. The teeth should be alternately set, or bent, toward either side of the sawplate, so the saw won't bind in the cut. But make sure there's not too much set or the saw will rattle around in the cut. I like my saws set about the thickness of a playing card or two on each side.

If your saw needs sharpening, you can send it out to be sharpened, but be cautious of commercial sharpeners who deal mostly with table saw blades and router bits. Many of them are clueless when it comes to sharpening handsaws and may do more harm than good.

Instead, seek out someone who special-izes in sharpening handsaws. Better yet, learn to sharpen and set them yourself.

Second, ditch your pencil and get a marking knife, at least for crosscuts. Using a knife instead of a pencil for crosscuts has two advantages. First, by marking the cutline on all four sides of the board with a knife, you reduce the chipping and tearing on the exit side of the cut. Second, if you knife your lines deep and start your saw relatively close to the knife line, the first stroke of the saw will break out the fibers on the waste side of the knife line and the saw will "jump" over right up against the shoulder. This makes accurately start-ing the cut much easier.

Last, look at your sawbench. If you don't already have a proper sawbench, what are you waiting for? No shop should be without a pair of sawbenches. You'll find several good designs in this book (see pages 102, 105, and 108). Pick one and build it.

WORK WITH YOUR BODY, NOT AGAINST IT

Believe it or not, our brains have a fairly precise built-in level. However, if we don't position our bodies to use this internal level to our advantage, it can work against us and lead our saw cuts astray.

When we set up to begin saw-ing, whether at the vise or over the sawbench, body position has a lot to do with how the final cut will come out. Our brains naturally want to follow a straight line. To use this to our advan-tage, we need to line up with the cutline correctly, even if the cutline is not per-pendicular to the board face (such as when sawing dovetail pins).

As a right-handed sawyer, if you close your left eye and look only through your right eye, the only thing you should see is the back of the saw (reverse this for southpaws). If you're

Test for sharpness. If the teeth don't grab the skin of your flattened palm when you try to gently (emphasis on "gently") move the saw across it, it's not really sharp.

Make ready. To saw accu-rately, grip the handle with a three-fingered grip, point your index finger at the toe of the saw, line up your arm and shoulder with the cutline, and position your eye directly above the saw.

positioned properly and you can see the side of the sawplate through your right eye, the cut is not plumb.

This natural tendency for the brain to line everything up can work against us if we don't line up properly with the cutline. If we were to stand slightly to the left of the cutline, for example, the natural tendency for the brain to line everything up would cause us to pull the heel of the saw out of square and

tilt the top of the saw out of plumb. To counter this, we fight our internal level in order to try and follow the line. However, sawing this way is rarely successful or consistent.

GETTING BACK ON TRACK

Even if we position ourselves correctly (or think we did), miscuts can still happen. When a cut begins to go awry, immediately stop. To get back on track, first re-adjust your body position in relation to the cutline. Then lower the angle of attack of the saw to the face of the board. Doing so lengthens the kerf and permits minor corrections to the course. Once the cutline has been corrected and is back on track, raise the saw back up and continue cutting along the line.

PERFECT PRACTICE

A great way to practice these sawing mechanics is to make the crosscuts and rips for the secondary parts of your projects, such as drawer sides, bottoms and case backs, using your handsaws. These parts are typically made of softer woods such as pine and poplar, which are easy to saw. These secondary parts also aren't typically seen in the finished piece, so mistakes are easily hidden.

Even if you aren't a hand-tool junkie, sawing with long handsaws once in awhile is the best way to develop the hand-eye coordination and muscle memory needed to become a better sawyer. Practicing good mechanics with longer saws and longer cuts is a skill that directly transfers to your joinery saws, and can help to vastly improve your hand-cut joinery. You may even find it kind of fun!

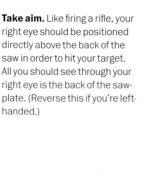
Take aim. Like firing a rifle, your right eye should be positioned directly above the back of the saw in order to hit your target. All you should see through your right eye is the back of the sawplate. (Reverse this if you're left-handed.)

Low and long. Drop the heel of the saw to lengthen the kerf and correct a cut that begins to drift.

SAW SHARPENING 101

A well-tuned tool pays great dividends when the blade hits the board.

BY MATT CIANCI

We've all been there: You reach for your saw in the middle of a project, and before you start the cut, you drag your finger along the teeth and say to yourself, "Meh... they're sharp enough." You soon find out they are anything but.

Wouldn't it be nice if you could sharpen your own saws and never have to settle for the misery of a dull saw again? With a small investment of time and money, you can.

So let's jump right into the four critical steps to sharpening any handsaw: setting, jointing, filing, and stoning.

SETTING

A saw's set—the right and left projection of the teeth from the sawplate—determines the width of the kerf and prevents the saw from binding.

Setting the teeth might not always be needed, so the first step is to evaluate.

To test your saw's set, make a cut in a piece of wood that is a species, thickness, and moisture content typical of your work. If the saw binds (gets stuck in the cut), it requires setting. If the blade is loose in the kerf, however, then it may be over-set, which can be corrected in the final step of stoning.

Most saw set tools adjust to allow setting different sizes of teeth and types of work. I recommend adjusting your tool to create the slightest amount of set for a backsaw, and only a touch more for a handsaw. Ignore the numbers on the tool; they are there only to confuse you.

If your saw requires setting, begin by clamping the saw in a vise with the toothline about 2" above the jaws. Starting at the heel of the saw, identify the first tooth set away from you. Place the

Rip teeth vs. crosscut teeth. Rip teeth (left) are shaped like tiny chisels and are shaped and sharpened by filing square across the blade. Crosscut teeth are shaped more like knives and are formed by filing at an angle to the blade.

THE SAW FILING TOOLS YOU NEED

Taper saw files (and handle): Match the tooth spacing of your saw to the properly sized file. Always use the properly sized handle.

- 12 to 15 ppi: 4" or 5" double-extra-slim taper (xx-slim)
- 10 to 11 ppi: 6" double-extra-slim taper (xx-slim)
- 9 ppi: 6" extra-slim taper (x-slim)
- 8 ppi: 6" slim taper
- 5 to 7 ppi: 7" slim taper
- 3.5 to 4.5 ppi: 7" regular taper

Mill file: Bastard cut, 6" to 8" for backsaws, 10" to 12" for handsaws.
Saw set: Any brand or style will work, though there are no quality new saw sets made today.
Saw vise: Shop-made of wood for the thrifty (see page 116), purchased for the demanding, or vintage cast iron for the nostalgic. I file for two to four hours every day and there is no equal to my Gramercy.
Sharpening stone: 6" x 2" #600-grit diamond stone or fine India stone for handsaws, 1" x 4" stone for backsaws.
Saw filing guide: I prefer shop-made wooden guides for rake and bevel angles because they are free when made from scraps, as well as light and endlessly customizable. That said, purchased guides are very helpful to students.

Set. Slip the saw set over the saw blade, rest it firmly on the toothline, align the hammer with a sawtooth, then squeeze.

Mill files

Tapered saw files

Saw vise

Handle

Sharpening stone

Saw set

Bevel angle guides

Rake angle guides

Joint. A file (held here in a shop-made saw jointing guide) levels the teeth to one another and creates a flat top on each. (You can purchase a similar jointing guide; search for "card scraper jointing guide" online.)

saw set so the center of the hammer (the steel mechanism that bends the tooth over the anvil) aligns with the point of the tooth. Make sure the casting rests solidly on the toothline and squeeze the tool firmly. You will see the tooth bend ever so slightly away from you. Skip the next tooth and move on to the next tooth set away from you. Set it as you did before, and repeat down the entire length of the saw. Flip the saw around in the vise and set the teeth you skipped on the first pass.

JOINTING

Jointing a saw every time you sharpen it ensures that the teeth are all the same height. It also creates a flat facet at the very point of each tooth that will guide your work in the filing step.

To begin jointing, keep the saw firmly in the vise with about 2" of the blade above the jaws. Grasp the mill file with both hands and rest it on the toothline at the heel. Run the file down the toothline toward the toe of the saw, using moderate pressure, until you see a flat facet on the point of each tooth. Two to four passes of the file should be sufficient for most saws.

It is critical that you keep the file perpendicular to the side of the saw blade as you joint the teeth. You can use a card scraper jointing guide or a block of wood to aid in this process.

Before you move on to filing the teeth, attach a rake-angle guide to the tip of the file to create consistent geometry on the cutting face of each tooth. Most rip-filed saws have a tooth rake of 5° to 10°, and most crosscuts have 15°.

A rake guide is a small block of wood, or a commercially made affair with moving parts, knurling, and scales galore, that slips over the tip of the file to create a visual reference for the rake angle as you file. If you make your own, you'll need one for each size of file and rake angle you typically use.

TERMINOLOGY

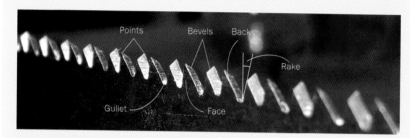

There is much confusion around terms associated with saw filing. It is important to use standardized and accurate language when teaching or learning a new skill, especially one as ancient as saw filing. These are the historically accurate and best terms to use.

- **Spacing:** The American standard measure of tooth points per inch (ppi)— just the points—on any saw that determines its coarseness or fineness. The English standard uses teeth per inch (tpi)—measuring entire teeth— which is equal to points per inch minus one. So 6 ppi equals 5 tpi. Tooth spacing is often incorrectly referred to as "pitch" by modern saw manufacturers, and many use ppi and tpi interchangeably.
- **Rake:** The amount that the front-cutting face of a saw tooth leans back from perpendicular relative to the toothline. Measured in degrees from the perpendicular. Also traditionally referred to as "pitch."
- **Bevel:** The interior acute angle on the face and point of a saw tooth that creates a cutting edge for cross-grain cuts. Also commonly referred to as "fleam."
- **Gullet:** The V-shaped space between two neighboring saw teeth where the sawdust collects in use.

RIP SAW FILING

The goal in this step is to file each tooth until the flat created by jointing disappears—and not a stroke more. The moment the flat disappears is the moment that the tooth is sharp and remains exactly the same height as the rest of the teeth. (Were you to continue filing, the tooth would stay sharp, but get shorter than the others, rendering it useless.)

Clamp the saw in the vise with the heel on your right and the bottom of the gullets ⅛" above the jaws. Place the saw file in the first gullet. Ensure the file is seated fully in the bottom of the gullet. Hold the file perpendicular to the side of the saw blade (level with the floor) and

Rip-tooth geometry. A rip saw is filed to form a row of tiny scrapers. The moment the flat formed by jointing is filed away, the saw is sharp.

ON DOING IT WRONG

There are warnings in classic saw filing texts about sharpening entirely from one side. While I am usually deferent to wisdom of the past, I deviate from it here. Why? I honestly don't recall; it's simply the way I learned to file a saw. Many others today also file all from one side. You should be aware of this debate if you plan on sharpening your own saws. Here are the major objections:

1 Filing from one side of the saw dulls the file faster because you have to file into the teeth leaning toward you, which causes more wear on the file teeth.
The gullet edge of the file is what wears out first and destroys a file. I find the extra wear to the face edges rather irrelevant; they stay intact long after the file is useless, regardless of how you file teeth.

2 Filing from one side of a saw alone puts all of the filing burrs on the opposite side of the saw teeth and will cause the cut to steer to that side when the saw is used.
I have filed hundreds of saws. The only case in which I've found the above to be true is in dovetail saws and similar saws spaced 14 ppi or finer. The fine teeth can be affected

by the burr, but an extra stoning pass or two on the burr side of the teeth is a simple remedy. On saws with teeth coarser than 14 ppi, I've found they are large enough to overcome any problems a burr might create.

3 You cannot create saw teeth with independently shaped back bevels (sloped gullets) by filing from one side of the saw.
I would say this is mostly true. But for 95 percent of woodworkers, I don't think independent back bevels on the teeth make a difference. For most work, the benefit is negligible. Can you gain a small advantage in your work with independently shaped back bevels? Sure. But to me, it's like the difference between a Corvette and a Ferrari.

So with all of these objections, you may be wondering why don't I just flip the saw, file from either side and avoid the controversy? For that matter, why do some people cut the pins of their dovetails first? Or use sandpaper after smoothing with a handplane? Or do any of the seemingly strange things that any of us do a million times a day?

Like most things in life, I simply have no idea. But I do know my method works.

Watch the angle.
The angle at which you push the file across the teeth affects the saw's cutting geometry.

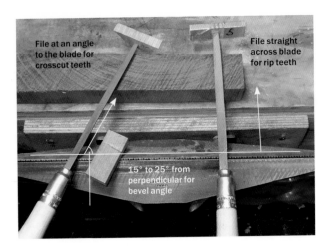

File at an angle to the blade for crosscut teeth

File straight across blade for rip teeth

15° to 25° from perpendicular for bevel angle

to the toothline as viewed from above. Use the full length of the file and push it across the saw with gentle pressure.

Beginning filers have a tendency to use short, heavy, chattering strokes. Light, full, even strokes are the mark of an accomplished and precise saw filer. When you push the file across the

saw you should see bright, fresh steel exposed on three surfaces: the cutting face of the tooth to the right of the file, the gullet, and the back face of the tooth on the left of the file.

Continue filing across the tooth while watching the flat on the right of the file. Stop filing the precise moment that the flat on the right of the file disappears. Move to the next gullet and continue the same process down the entire length of the saw on every tooth.

CROSSCUT SAW FILING

After jointing the saw, reclamp it, again with the bottom of the gullets about 1/16" above the vise jaws, and place the saw file in between the first pair of teeth at the heel, with a tooth set toward you on the right of the file and a tooth set away from you to the left. This may be either the first or second gullet on the toothline.

With the file resting in the gullet and using your index finger on the file where it rests on the saw, press the file firmly down into the gullet. The file should rotate away from a perpendicular line from the saw as viewed from above, usually 15° to 25° for most crosscut saws. This is the bevel angle of the teeth. Filing at this angle creates the knife edge that allows the saw teeth to cut across the grain of wood fibers.

Take your first stroke with the file fully seated in the gullet while carefully maintaining the bevel angle, and watch the flat on both teeth to the right and the left of the file. The goal is to file until you have simultaneously reduced the width of the flat on both teeth by half.

Skip the next gullet and move to the following gullet with a tooth set toward you on the right of the file. Now repeat the process of filing while maintaining the bevel angle and watching both teeth on either side of the file. Reduce the flats on both teeth by half and stop. Skip the next gullet and repeat as you make your way down the saw.

As you progress, observe the pattern of every pair of teeth filed in one direction with every other gullet not yet filed.

Once you have filed each pair of teeth in one direction down the length of the saw, return to the heel.

Now you'll remove the flats left from the previous step to bring all the teeth to a sharp edge. Place the file in the first gullet at the heel you skipped earlier. The tooth set away from you should be on the left of the file and the tooth set toward you should be on the right.

As before, press the file down into the gullet and notice how the file's angle rotates away from perpendicular—but in the opposite direction as before. This angle should be the same relative angle from perpendicular as before, (15° to 25°). This final angle filed into each tooth will create the second and complemen-tary interior bevel and complete the crosscut geometry.

As before, while maintaining a consistent bevel angle, push the file through the gullet and watch both flats on either side of the file. Keep the file seated in the gullet and ensure that you are removing metal from the face of each tooth in addition to the gullet. Ideally, you want each flat to disappear at the same moment. This ensures that each tooth is sharp and of equal height.

Continue to the next unfiled gullet and repeat filing each pair of teeth until you complete the saw.

STONING

The final step in sharpening a saw is to stone it. Place the tool flat on your bench with the handle overhanging the edge. With a fine India stone or 600-grit diamond stone, use light pressure as you run the stone along the teeth down the length of the saw to even the set and remove the burrs created by filing. Flip the saw over and repeat. One pass per side is sufficient. (If the saw was over-set to begin with, take more strokes as required.) No more than four strokes per side is recommended. (This step is also known as "side jointing.")

You may find in a test cut after sharpening a fine rip-filed saw (14 ppi and up) that it steers to one side. This is a common result from a burr on the teeth left from filing only from one side. To remedy this, take an extra stoning pass on the side toward which the saw is steering. This will remove the burr and even the cut in the kerf.

Sure, like everything, saw filing takes a bit of practice to get good at, but it doesn't take too much time or effort to become at least competent. Take the time to learn how to sharpen your own saws, and you'll be amazed at how much better they work—and how much time and money you'll save over sending them out for sharpening.

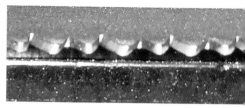

Crosscut tooth geometry. Jointing crosscut saw teeth creates triangular flats at the point of each tooth. These reflect light and help guide the sharpening process.

Stoning. To remove burrs left by the filing, and to remove set, make no more than four passes down each side of the teeth with a fine India stone or 600-grit diamond stone.

3

SPECIALTY SAWS

Move beyond traditional handsaws and backsaws. Now that you understand the basics and techniques of using handsaws and backsaws, it's time to delve into specialty handsaws. The bow saw is a classic hand tool that played a large role in the creation of most early-American furniture and is a suitable replacement for the bandsaw. Coping saws are perfect for scrollwork, once appropriately adapted; flush-cut saws are useful for finishing off pegs.

THE FORGOTTEN MITER BOX

Once common, the miter box has been relegated to garage sales; here's why you should find one for your workshop.

BY RON HERMAN

I build houses for a living, and I have a full array of power equipment at my disposal. Yet, when I trim out a house or construct built-ins, I almost always turn to one of my manual miter boxes.

These nearly forgotten tools are more accurate than power saws. They can handle stock and moldings that many power saws struggle with. And they are cheap, rugged, and hiding under every rock (if you know where to look).

In fact, miter boxes have always been a staple of my family's construction business, and I think they should be in your workshop as well. So here's an introduction to one of my favorite tools.

TYPES OF MITER BOXES

There are several types of miter boxes that you'll find in the wild. The simplest type is an open wooden trough with metal or wooden guides. These are usually craftsman made, sometimes with commercially made metal parts. Though you can do good work with these boxes, you can easily find more advanced models.

A second type of box is a metal table with a fence at the back. There is a single pivoting post at the fence that guides a saw back and forth. These miter boxes are usually designed for panel saws or handsaws, though they can also accommodate a backsaw. Many people call this form an "open-front" miter box. The

Still on the job. Miter boxes work just as well today as they did when they built this country. With a little patience you can find one (or seven) that will serve you for the rest of your life.

A simple box. A miter box can be as rudimentary as a U-shaped trough. This one has some commercial metal guides added to it to improve its accuracy.

Open-front box. Here's an open-front miter box equipped with a panel saw. These are superior to simple miter boxes and have a huge crosscutting capacity.

Open wide. Miter boxes can have an enormous capacity. And their cuts are unmatched for accuracy and safety.

The full enchilada. This fully framed miter box has all the bells and whistles, including a system to hold the blade locked above your work when you're not using it. This is the most accurate style of box.

A special feature. Some miter boxes allow you to move one of the posts forward toward the operator in order to increase the maximum cutting width of the miter box.

No degrees. Some early boxes didn't mark the angles in degrees. Instead, they marked the quadrant with the number of sides that would be created with that angle setting. Set the box to "4" and you will get a four-sided frame (it's 45°). Set it to "6" and you'd create a six-sided frame (it's 30°).

A little grabby. One feature on certain boxes is a stitched table. These tiny stitches grab your work and hold it fast.

advantage of these boxes is that you can saw really wide stuff if need be—just get a bigger saw.

The third type of box is a "fully framed" miter box. It also has a metal L-shaped frame. But instead of one guide, it has two: one guide at the fence and one up by the user. These miter boxes are almost always designed for a backsaw. And when set up correctly, the saw slides back and forth as smooth as silk, and it makes perfect straight or mitered cuts.

This type of miter box also can have a lot of gizmos for making repetitive cuts of all the same length or even cutting tenon shoulders to a preset depth. The

fully framed box is probably the one that most furniture makers should keep an eye out for.

BUT WHICH BOX?

Though there were a number of companies that made miter boxes, you're mostly going to find ones made by Stanley or Millers Falls (which will sometimes be branded as Acme or Langdon). I use both brands in my work; both can be fine tools.

If pressed, I usually recommend woodworkers get the Millers Falls boxes if they have a choice. Millers Falls didn't change its components much over the years. So if you ever need parts for

them, they will be easier to come by on "donor" boxes and will most likely fit like a glove. One weakness of the Millers Falls boxes is the spring that locks the angle of the saw. It tends to rust.

The Stanley boxes can also be great (as long as they aren't plastic). However, Stanley made so many different models and types with different parts that it can be hard to find replacement parts.

No matter what the brand, miter box saws come in many sizes, from the tiny Langdon No. 16½ with a 16"-long saw with a 2" depth of cut, all the way up to the monster Langdon Acme No. 75 with a 30"-long saw with a full 5" depth of cut (heck Stanley even made saws with a

Great for tenons. The secondary depth stops on many good miter boxes allow you to temporarily set the cutting depth. These are great for cutting tenon shoulders.

That's not a hang hole. Some miter saws have a hole in the back at the end of the toe. If you insert a nail or a cotter pin it will prevent you from pulling the saw out of the box on the return stroke.

Other gizmos. You'll see these bars on some miter boxes. They are designed to help hold your crown against the fence while you make a cut.

6" depth of cut). My work falls typically in the middle range. I prefer a 26"-long saw that has a 4" depth of cut for most trimming chores. If you deal with small moldings or rails and stiles, you might look for a smaller box.

AND WHAT TYPE OF SAW?

First off, I recommend you learn to sharpen your own saws. Many woodworkers I see with these boxes have a saw that's so dull it couldn't cut butter if it fell on it. When you sharpen a saw for a miter box, joint the snot out of the teeth. Every tooth has to be at the same height because every tooth has to do its job in a miter box. Second tip: I don't usually file a sloping gullet with my handsaws or backsaw, but I'll file sloping gullets on my miter saws. The deeper gullets seem to hold more sawdust.

Most miter saws will be sharpened crosscut with about 11 points per inch (ppi). This is a good general filing, though I like to use a finer pitch (such as 13 ppi) with harder woods such as oak, and a coarser pitch if I'm working with a lot of soft pine. I even keep some miter saws filed for ripping with 9 ppi. I use these for trimming rosettes when I have

to cut them with the grain. And sometimes you'll set a miter box to 60° and the cut is a lot more like a rip. But I have a lot of saws.

WHERE TO FIND THEM

Miter saws were in the truck of every carpenter and in the garage of many homeowners—until the powered miter saws took over. There are millions of manual miter boxes out there. However, because they are heavy and difficult to ship, you don't see them show up for sale much online.

As a result, you have to hit the streets. Attend a few auctions and you'll see them come up. I find lots of them at garage sales and flea markets. They even show up at tool swaps that are sponsored by tool collecting associations (such as the Mid-West Tool Collectors Association). However, few tool collectors are interested in common usergrade miter boxes.

Put the word out in your neighborhood and with your friends that you are looking for one. Lots of people have them deep in their basement or garage.

HOW TO USE THEM

We always mount our miter saws to a piece of plywood or scrap that has a cleat on its front edge. This allows us to hook them onto a flat surface (like a bench hook) when we're in the field. If your miter box is going to stay in the shop you can set up your box so that it drops into dog holes on your bench. Or you can pinch the wooden plate between dogs with a vise. No matter which way you go, you'll find sawing easier if the box is secure.

If you are a good sawyer, then the actual cut is fairly straightforward. The first thing to do is to make sure all the box's depth settings are correct. You want the saw to stop cutting right as the teeth slice through the work that's against the table. This reduces the

Not too deep. The depth stops on a miter saw are a critical setting. Set them too shallow and you won't cut through your work. Set them too deep and you could destroy your saw.

The correct setting. The teeth should float right above the metal guide below when the saw is at full depth.

Just like sawing. Allow your arm to swing free when you saw with a miter box. And use as much of the length of the sawplate as you can.

tearing you'll get on the back side of your work. You also don't want the teeth to drag against the metal parts of the frame.

I typically start by dropping the blade on the work to confirm it's right where I want it. Then I begin the cut on the corner of the work against the fence using no downward pressure on the saw. Watch the kerf and ensure you are cutting square. If you are aggressive you will move the saw off the line.

Once I have the kerf established then I can switch to sawing with my arm like a locomotive linkage—back and forth in a straight line. Use as much of the saw as you can. When I finish the cut, I want to have to press down just a little bit to slice through the last of the fibers. Try it, and I think you'll agree.

And once you've used a miter box with a sharp saw and correct technique, I think you'll be sold. In fact I think I'll start seeing you at the garage sales and auctions that I haunt. Watch yourself—I'm an early riser.

BOW SAW BASICS

This ancient European tool still has a place in the modern American shop.

BY FRANK KLAUSZ

Why should you own a bow saw? Why not? You have many other tools that you use only when you need them. Seriously, if you make 18th-century-style furniture, or you make furniture with hand tools, you should own a couple of bow saws.

In my shop, which has all the machines you can imagine, I use bow saws. If I cut dovetails in material thicker than ½", I reach for my bow saw. I keep my material behind my shop in a pole barn. If I have to crosscut a board for one piece, the fastest way is with a bow saw. I put the board on a couple horses, cut it, put the leftover back on the rack and take the piece in the shop. There's no extension cord or machine to put away.

In my native Hungary, I grew up without electricity. Therefore in the

(Above) An old friend. When my father came to the United States for a visit, I was reintroduced to a saw that once was my "go to" saw in woodworking. My bow saw quickly reclaimed that exalted status.

shop, the bow saw was the main tool used for crosscuts, rips, dovetails, mortise-and-tenon joinery, and more.

My father came for a visit to the United States in 1974, and he spent some time working with me in my shop. He started looking for the frame saws. I told him, "Sorry Dad, this is America; we cut wood with machines."

A year later he came for another visit and brought a dozen different bow saw blades: 5 teeth per inch (tpi) for ripping, 4 tpi for rough crosscutting, 12 tpi for joinery, and a dovetail cutout saw—which is a blade with a 90° twist in it. He made frames, handles, stretchers, and toggles and used upholstery twine (look for "Ruby Italian" twine from an upholstery supplier) for tensioning the blades with toggles. He kept a saw close at hand, sometimes hanging it on a peg next to the bench. We did furniture restorations, and he used the saws very often.

He said to me: "By the time you walk to the bandsaw, before you start it, I am done with the cut, very comfortably, without going to the middle of the shop. For a corner block or a ⅜" dowel rod, you don't start a machine. The corner block you cut with a bow saw; the ⅜" dowel rod you cut with your small dovetail saw."

This year I am the same age as my father was in 1975, and I truly agree with him.

JAPANESE TEETH; EUROPEAN FRAME

Recently, I got a classic frame saw from Highland Woodworking. They put a Japanese blade onto a classic European saw frame. This German-made classic frame saw's ergonomically curved cheeks and handles are made from plantation-grown tropical hardwoods, and the stretcher is made from cedar, which makes it lightweight.

The frame is beautifully sanded and finished. Tension is applied through a stainless steel rod and thumbscrew, which works very well. However, I changed mine to the traditional twine and toggle. This looks and feels better and is very easy to tension and to relieve the tension before hanging it up. The saw is light and fits in your hand very comfortably.

The heart and soul of this saw is its impulse-hardened Japanese blade. The tooth profile allows fast, clean cutting in any direction with very little set to the teeth. The 12 tpi "Turbo-Cut" blade cuts faster than my 5 tpi blade. I cut a 10"-wide, 1"-thick mahogany board very

A time and back saver. It's much easier to take a bow saw to your lumber than it is to drag the stock into the shop. And, there's no hassle with extension cords.

easily and with a comfortable pace in less than 10 seconds with 10 to 11 strokes. This frame saw, called the "Classic 700" is 39" long. They also make a "Classic 400," which is 26½" long. I recommend the 700 for ripping and crosscutting and for large tenoning, and the 400 for all other joinery.

Old methods work best. New bow saws are tensioned with a rod and thumbscrews, but I prefer twine and a toggle. The loose end is wrapped around and through the twine to hold it in place.

Check the tension. I determine the correct tension by holding the saw by the toggle to see how it hangs; also by how well the saw cuts. It's easy to adjust tension with a twist of the toggle.

It's hip. A bow saw makes quick work of ripping stock for your project. As you finish the cut, catch it with your hip. After a couple swings, it's a natural motion.

A sum of all parts. A bow saw is made with simple parts and basic joinery, but when assembled, you have a workhorse of a saw.

A great saw for detail work. A 12" bow saw set up with a fine blade increases your control and produces a finer cut, such as when you are cutting dovetails.

A SMALLER BOW SAW

I also got a 12" bow saw from Gramercy Tools. It is beautifully made and has a small frame. Three different blades are included with the saw. There is an all-purpose 18 tpi blade. For rough work or thick material, change to the 10 tpi blade. The 24 tpi blade will be the most useful on thin stock and fine, slow cuts.

To change a blade, loosen the tension on the saw by unwinding the toggle, then simply unhook the blade and hook on another. Position the blade so that it will cut on the push stroke. Because the blades have cross pins they are easy to change and great for swinging in and out of pierced work. After changing blades, re-tension the saw by twisting the toggle.

I use the 12" bow saw instead of a coping saw. It cuts much faster. I use it to cut out my pins and tails close to the marking-gauge line when I am dovetailing and I clean up with a chisel.

Whatever saw you are getting, be patient and cut with a gentle push and long strokes. With a little practice, it becomes part of you and much easier to control than other saws.

BOW SAW TECHNIQUES

Discover the ins and outs of this versatile saw.

BY MICHAEL DUNBAR

In the 1970s when I was the young, innocent, and naive chairmaker at Strawbery Banke, a museum in Portsmouth, N.H., 50,000 tourists passed through my shop each summer. It never failed that when I was cutting out a chair seat with a bow saw some wag would quip loudly, "You need a bandsaw!"

While these comics guffawed at their own cleverness, I was puzzled by the comment's inanity. I knew I was doing just fine and didn't need a bandsaw. I did my work quickly and efficiently with two different-sized bow saws—large and small. The saws did all the work I required. I cut out two chair seats a week and four scrolled hands. If the chair had a crest, I cut that too.

The saws cost very little, relative to a bandsaw. When I was done, I hung them on the wall, where they took up no floor space in my cramped shop. I was perfectly happy working this way.

After I had grown up and started demonstrating at woodworking shows, I continued to get the same comment from woodworkers who, carried away with their own wittiness, could not stop themselves from blurting, "You need a bandsaw!" It was then that I realized everyone thought I should have a bandsaw because they didn't know about

Put a bow saw to work. Many modern woodworkers avoid bow saws because they don't understand when or how to use them in the shop.

bow saws. It was their loss. They missed out on the enjoyment of using a very efficient tool that has been around since the Bronze Age and was used in Europe and America to produce the great 18th-century furniture masterpieces we go to museums to admire.

MEET THE BOW SAW, MODERNER

In the history of woodworking there were many types of bow saws, some developed by tradesmen to meet their own particular needs. For example, inlay makers cut out very small pieces with a fret saw, while wheelwrights cut out sections for wooden wheels (fellows) with a fellow saw. Today, we use far fewer bow saws, but these share a number of features with all their ancestors. First is a thin blade that conserves steel and allows the bow saw to change directions more easily than would be permitted by a wide-bladed handsaw. Second is a wooden frame that secures the blade. Third are the handles, which provide the user with something to hold, and which can be turned to adjust the direction of cut. Finally, every bow saw has some method that tensions the blade—that is, stretches it tight.

For general woodworking—the sort of things most of us do—you need only two bow saws. A large saw with about a 25"-long blade is great for ripping or cutting shapes out of heavy stock. A smaller saw with about a 12" blade is better for cutting out smaller parts.

The biggest obstacle you face in adding bow saws to your repertoire of woodworking skills is obtaining one. A lot of woodworking catalogs and web sites sell bow saws, but beware: Most of these saws are cheaply made, lightweight, and inadequate for woodworking. The same rule that applies to the lathe and workbench applies to the bow saw: Flimsy equals worthless.

Why? Sawing requires force. The reason my large bow saw is so efficient

Toggle the tension. A toggle such as this allows you to adjust the frame's tension by half-turns, which is better for the saw.

Get a grip. When ripping, grasp the strut with one hand and the handle with the other. Begin your kerf with the lower part of the blade engaged in the wood.

Use your whole body. When using the large saw like this, don't use only your arms. Use the mass of your body to help bring the saw down. Flex your knees and bend slightly at the waist.

It tracks tightly. While the surface from a bow saw might be rough, I find a bow saw is easier to keep from drifting off line than a bandsaw.

Rip away. When you are ripping with the large saw, tilt the frame away from you slightly to help stay on your line.

is that I can put a lot of weight and muscle behind it without the saw flexing or the frame wiggling. If either of these happens, the cutting action is less effective and the saw is harder to direct. My prejudice against commercial bow saws is well founded. I have had one fall apart in my hands while cutting a chair seat.

HERE'S A GOOD BOW SAW

These are the criteria to look for in a saw. You want a rigid hardwood frame, which will give the saw serious heft. The strut should attach to the ends with mortise-and-tenon joints. These should be deep and well fit, with no play or slop. You want the handle rods to be metal (usually brass). The rods should have a tight friction fit where they pass through the frame to secure the blade, so the blade cannot turn while in use. In other words, adjusting the saw should require effort. The blade should be secured to the rods by a slot pierced by a metal pin. All these parts should be robust enough not to wear or break. The strut and handles should be designed for comfort and have smooth relieved corners that will not raise blisters. I particularly like octagonal handles on my saws.

You have to be able to tension or stretch the blade so it does not flex or twist. Most saws are tensioned by twisting a hank of string with a wooden toggle. I do not like wire that is tightened with a nut. This mechanism is not as effective. For string, I recommend waxed cobbler's twine. It holds up well to years of use and does not stretch.

Most saws use a simple stick as a toggle for twisting and tightening the twine. Overlapping the toggle on the center strut keeps the twine from unwinding. However, the tighter you twist the twine, the tighter it becomes on the toggle. At some point the toggle will not slide at all and you can no longer tension the saw by full turns. This can be a problem, because over tightening can

break the frame. The answer is the yoke with a sliding toggle as shown at the top of page 81.

The grooved yoke fits into the twisted rope, allowing the slotted toggle to slide freely. You can make full or half turns without any fuss.

Because most commercial bow saws are inadequate, you are faced with either making your own or buying one from a craftsman/maker. A bow saw requires only several small pieces of hardwood, so it is a good project for using up some cutoffs or scrap.

THE RIGHT BLADES

The type of blade you choose to mount in your saw is determined by your intended use for the tool. I use my large bow saw most frequently for cutting out chair seats. This means I am driving it through nearly 2" of pine. I want my blade to be aggressive and fast. I don't care if the cut leaves a coarse surface. When I am done, I will shape the edge of the seat and remove all evidence of the sawing. I use a length of 6 points per inch (ppi) ⅜" bandsaw blade in the saw. Because I need the blade to be stiff and unflexible, I use a .035"-thick blade rather than the more common .025". You may not be able to buy this blade in your local woodworking store, but you can find it on the Internet. The blade on my small bow saw is a 16 ppi, ¼" saw blade.

If you make your own blades, you will have to drill holes for the pins that pass through the handle rods. The saw steel is too hard to drill, so soften the ends by heating them with a propane torch.

BENCH OR HORIZONTAL SAWING WITH THE LARGE SAW

The large bow saw cuts on the down, or push stroke, and the blade is mounted in this direction. The teeth are turned so they are at a right angle to the frame. A bow saw is a turning saw, which means the blade can be turned so it is at a set-

Straight through the curves. When you turn a corner, bring the frame up until it's vertical, which prevents the edge from becoming beveled.

ting other than 90° to the frame, but I seldom do this. If you do need to turn the blade, loosen the toggle and turn the upper and lower handles at the same time. If you turn them separately, you risk twisting or breaking the blade.

The large saw cuts with the stock secured to the benchtop, so your bench needs to be the right height for sawing. Most modern benches are too high for most hand tools, and certainly for the large bow saw. My test for proper bench height is to stand erect next to the bench with your arm straight and rigid at your side. Bend your hand at the wrist so it is parallel to the floor. The palm of your hand establishes the best height for your bench. If your bench is too high for the bow saw, either trim the legs or stand on a platform when sawing.

Secure the work to the bench with clamps that are heavy and strong enough to hold it fast. How you position the stock on the bench depends on the work. To be as efficient as possible, here are a couple things to consider before beginning. With the big saw, you travel along with the tool. Make sure you can move your body freely.

You do not want to stop and reposition your stock any more than is necessary. If you are ripping, clamp the stock to the bench so the kerf is close to the edge. This reduces any chance of the stock flexing. Short pieces and round shapes such as chair seats are easiest to cut with the stock clamped to a corner, although you will have to reposition the seat blank at least once. If in cutting a shape you have to cut around corners with a radius longer than your saw's throat, trim the corners first.

A bow saw has limitations. Like a bandsaw, its throat is only so wide. The maximum for my big saw is 6½". This means the saw works best for ripping narrow lengths and is useless when it comes to cutting plywood panels.

With the work secured, you are ready to use the saw. Hold the strut near the top with your dominant hand (I'm right-handed) and grip the upper handle with your other hand. Stand facing the direction of the cut, so the saw is in front of you.

Any hand-driven saw works best with a smooth stroke that uses almost the entire length of the blade. The same applies to a bow saw. With a large bow saw, the best advantage comes from using your entire body rather than your arms. Sawing is an aerobic exercise, and if done correctly you will not become fatigued or winded.

To prepare for the down stroke, raise the saw until the lower end of the blade is engaged on the line. As the saw descends, use the entire length of the blade, almost to the upper end. On the down stroke, come up slightly on your toes. Your heels will come off the floor. Flex your knees and bend slightly at the waist. This action, rather than your arms, is what moves the saw. While you cannot avoid some movement of your shoulders, it is surprising how little your arms are involved. Mostly, your arms and shoulders hold the saw in the cutting position while your body moves it. Raise the blade not with your arms, but by straightening your body and rocking your feet back flat on the floor.

You can understand the efficiency in this motion. Rather than trying to drive the saw with your arms and shoulders, you are putting the weight of your torso behind the blade.

At the end of the down stroke, pull the saw blade back slightly in the kerf. This accomplishes several things. First, the end of the kerf is tighter, so withdrawing the blade slightly makes it easier to lift the saw. Withdrawing the blade also clears trapped sawdust out of the kerf, especially at the end where you are cutting.

Armed with a small saw. When using the small bow saw, move your arms in a reciprocating fashion. Keep your torso steady.

Finally, withdrawing the blade makes sawing more accurate. Here's why. As you start the next down stroke, you reposition the blade on the line. Repeat this with every stroke. While this continuous correction will create a more ragged edge than that left by a bandsaw, an experienced bow saw-yer has less trouble with drifting off line. When you are done and examine the sawn edge, you can see where you started each stroke.

The key to using the bow saw efficiently is to make the movement repetitive and fluid. Any halting or jerkiness indicates you are doing something wrong. Once you have achieved skill with the tool, you will be amazed at how efficient and fast a bow saw is.

When ripping with the large bow saw, hold the saw so the frame is tilted away from you. Because it's on a diagonal, more of the blade is in the kerf, and it is easier to stay on the line. The kerf's leading edge—below the surface—is angled and still aligned with the line you are following.

As you cut a curve, bring the frame into vertical, so it is cutting in the same

manner as a bandsaw. If you tilt the frame as you do when ripping, the cut around the curve will be beveled, rather than at a right angle to the surface.

VERTICAL OR VISE SAWING

The small saw is intended for detail work and cutting out small parts. It simply does not have the heft to cut heavy stock. As with the big saw, I generally position the blade at a right angle to the frame. Like a coping saw, this tool cuts on the pull stroke rather than on the push.

The pull-stroke grip requires holding the saw by both handles. Because your arm reaches over the work, it cannot be secured horizontally on a benchtop. Instead, the work is held vertically in a vise. With the small saw, you generally have to stop and adjust the work to give the saw access to more of the pattern, but this is a lot faster and easier than adjusting clamps.

Once again, the saw's action needs to be smooth and use as much of the blade length as practical. In use, the small saw's stroke is fast. Imagine yourself as a human scroll saw. Each pull stroke

cuts and advances the kerf. On the back stroke, lift the blade slightly and reset it on the line before the next cut.

Operating the small saw is the opposite of the larger. While the big saw uses your entire body but not your arms, the small saw uses just your arms and shoulders but not your body. Plant your feet and bend your knees to bring your shoulders down to the height of the work. Retain this position. Lock your wrists and move the saw with your elbows and shoulders.

STORAGE IS SIMPLE

When you are finished with a bow saw, release the tension on the blade. Turning the toggle backward one turn is sufficient. You don't want to loosen the frame so much that it falls apart. I store my saws by hanging them on the wall. However, bow saws lie flat and can be stored in a tool box. If you do this, find a way to protect the blade from other tools, and to protect you from it.

IMPROVE A COPING SAW

Your saw can work better by adding washers or by changing the way you saw.

BY CHRISTOPHER SCHWARZ

When I was a kid, the first saw I bought was a coping saw with a chrome frame and red-stained handle. For years I did everything with that saw—crosscuts, rips, curves, and even joints. But I made none of those cuts particularly well.

Part of the problem was that I was 11 years old. But part of it was the saw. I still own that saw—it's sitting in front of me now—and it simply will not tension a blade enough to prevent it from twisting. A good coping saw will keep the blade fixed at one position when fully tensioned and it will allow the blade to move freely for scrollwork when the tension is backed off.

If you've bought a coping saw sometime in the last 40 years, you probably have encountered the same problems that I did. While cutting, the blade at the toe rotates, while the blade at the heel stays stationary. This results in a poor cut and broken blades.

(Right) Around the bend. If your coping saw doesn't work how you think it should, it could be the saw.

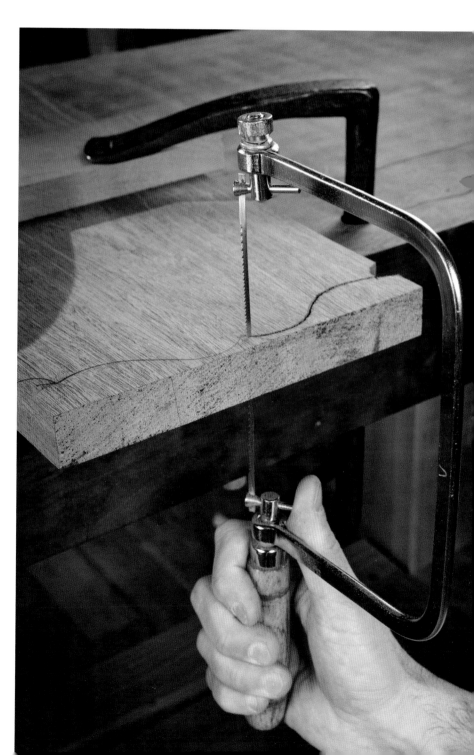

Twisted. The toe of my old coping saw tends to slip when I want it locked, even when the saw is fully tensioned. This makes the saw wander and produces an out-of-square cut.

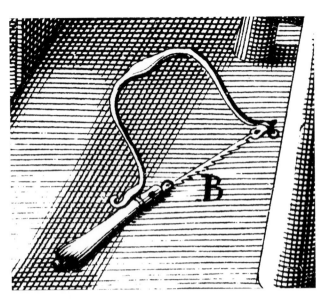

Not so different. This small frame saw from marquetry was shown in a 1676 French text on woodworking and architecture. It looks only slightly fancier than coping saws from today's home center.

Tighten it. Many saws rely on the frame alone to fix the blade in one position. Over time, the frame can become slack.

It wasn't always this way. Coping saws (and their ancestors) have a 500-year track record in woodworking. And after buying and using dozens of vintage coping saws, I have come to the conclusion that most of the modern ones aren't worth much. They don't tension the blade enough and their frames are weak at best. I know of three solutions:

1. Buy an expensive modern coping saw that actually tensions the blade.

2. Hunt down a well-made vintage coping saw with a stiff and well-tensioned frame.

3. Improve a cheap coping saw with some washers.

All three approaches are valid. But before diving into the nitty-gritty, I think it's important to understand where this ubiquitous woodworking saw came from. It has noble roots.

FROM THRONE ROOMS TO TOYS

While frame saws likely were invented by either the Romans or the Greeks, it wasn't until the Golden Age of veneered marquetry in the 16th century that the delicate bow saws required for the intricate work appeared. Several woodworking historians think marquetry

saws developed from the jeweler's saw, a small metal-framed saw used to cut precious materials.

In 1676, André Félibien published a drawing of a *petite sie de marqueterie* that looks for all the world like a modern coping saw—you can even see that the teeth point away from the handle (see image above). Furniture covered in marquetry was a favorite of royalty in mainland Europe and (by the 17th century) in England.

By the 18th century, these sorts of saws were sometimes called "Morris saws"—perhaps it was a bastardization of the word "Moorish," or it could relate to the inlaid game board for an old game called "Nine Men's Morris." These saws were used for all sorts of intricate cuts, both by cabinetmakers and jewelers. And the saws had blades designed to cut not only wood, but tortoiseshell, brass, and other semi-precious materials.

In the 19th century, the saws were commonly called "bracket saws," and during the middle part of the century a fretwork craze developed—you find advertisements for the saws and plans in publications that have nothing to do with woodwork, such as *The Pacific Tourist* and *Beautiful Homes* magazines.

Stop it. These saws have detents that keep the blade fixed at a certain number of positions.

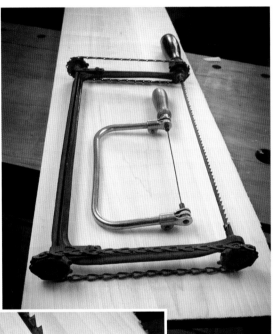

Spin it. Coping saws with pulleys keep the blade aligned no matter what sort of cutting you do. Sometimes they spin too much for waste removal, but you learn to control them.

Soon the saws spread to the schools, where 19th-century craft-based schools using the Sloyd system taught handwork that was based around using a knife, a "frame compass saw," and other simple tools to make toys. By the early 20th century, the saw had acquired its modern name, "coping saw," as carpenters found the tool handy for coping inside corners when cutting molding.

Historical purists might not agree that the coping saw is a descendant of the early marquetry saw, but from a user's perspective these saws are functional equivalents: a metal frame that tensions a thin blade that is used for curved and intricate cuts.

THREE WAYS TO FIX THE BLADE

While researching coping saws, I found three primary ways of keeping the blade aligned at both the toe and heel of the tool.

1. Tension alone. A lot of coping saws—good and bad—use the frame alone to tension the blade and fix it in one position. The two arms of the frame spread out so the opening for the blade is too big. You push the arms together to get the blade into the frame, which tensions the blade somewhat. And you can then increase the tension by turning the handle clockwise, which pulls the arms of the frame even closer together.

This works fine if the frame is rigid and keeps its original shape. Many coping saws with lightweight frames lose their shape after a few months. The arms bend in and stay bent. I have old saws from the early part of the 20th century that still tension the blade beautifully. So, some key metallurgical point has been forgotten or ignored.

2. Stops. Some saws have fixed detents or stops in the frame that help the blade stay aligned at the toe and heel. This solution can work brilliantly or not at all. Some modern coping saws have detents that are too shallow to

KNEW CONCEPTS—THE ALUMINUM CADILLAC

For those woodworkers who have prime-rib tastes, I recommend the Knew Concepts coping saw. It is astonishingly lightweight (8 ounces), tensions the blade to a high note, and can lock the blade in eight positions.

Except for the wooden handle, the tool's makers redesigned the tool from scratch. I've been using one for about 18 months and have zero complaints, except for the color. The factory red was just too much for me. So I painted it black to match my planes and my tool chest.

It is the most expensive coping saw on the market, but it also has no equal.

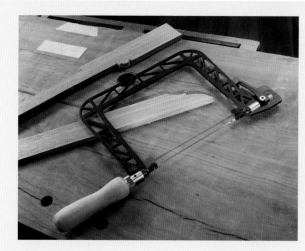

Modern technology. The Knew Concepts saw is different than traditional coping saws on almost every point.

hold anything—so you are back to relying on the frame alone to keep the blade fixed.

A downside to a saw with stops is that they don't always work well when you want the blade to rotate as you cut, such as when you are cutting curvaceous fretwork in thin materials. The stops are actually too aggressive. If you don't use your coping saw for fretwork, however, one of these saws is likely for you.

3. Pulleys. Some older coping saws that were designed for fretwork use an ingenious system of pulleys or rollers to keep the blade aligned at the toe and heel. One model uses a string that passes through the saw's frame to keep the blade aligned. Another type uses a chain. (Both are shown on page 87.)

These saws excel at coping fretwork—almost like magic. When using these to saw out dovetail waste, however, you need to pinch the handle and saw frame with your fingers to lock the blade's position.

A BARGAIN SOLUTION

Now you might be thinking that I'm going to send you on a wild goose chase for one of the aforementioned saws, which can be expensive, rare, or both. And that is certainly an option for people who like vintage or well-made tools.

But what if you just want a dang coping saw that works? For the last five years (at least), I've been fooling around with this idea, trying to find the best inexpensive coping saw and the simplest way to modify it to make it work well.

Here's the scoop: Buy an inexpensive coping saw (I recommend an Olson Deluxe Coping Saw). Right from the box, the Olson is a good saw. It's unique in that it has a locking mechanism at both the toe and heel. So you can get the blade to stay fairly aligned if you don't get too aggressive with it when cutting.

But with the addition of two pieces of cheap hardware from any hardware store, you can turn this saw into a blade-clamping monster. What you need are two 5/16" split washers, sometimes called "spring lock washers."

I have experimented with a lot of different kinds of washers, including wave washers and serrated-tooth washers. While these improve the saw, the wave washers wear out too quickly for my

taste, and the serrated-tooth washers prevent the blade from rotating in one direction only.

With the washers in place (see pictures above right), your saw is ready to go. You should be able to lock the blade so it might require pliers to move. That's great for cleaning out dovetail waste. Remove the washers, and the blade will rotate easily for scrollwork.

CHOOSING BLADES

Coping saws come in a variety of tooth configurations. You can get them with different teeth per inch (tpi). The typical range is 10 tpi up to 20 tpi. I use the 10-tpi blades for waste removal and usually a 15- or 18-tpi blade for scrollwork. If the material is thick, consider a skip-tooth blade. The wide spaces between the teeth prevent the blade's gullets from filling with sawdust.

I wish that coping saws didn't have so much set to the teeth, but there is little you can do about that with typical workshop equipment.

The hardware-store varieties are usually overset and break easily. A good-quality blade lasts longer and

Add split washers. A common coping saw comes with a plain washer between the handle and the saw frame. Remove it and replace it with a ⁵⁄₁₆" split washer (left). Then add a split washer between the screw at the toe and the frame (right).

Simple and cheap is best. The simple split steel washer works better in a coping saw than the fancier serrated-tooth washers or bronze cut washers.

makes sawing smoother. And just like with your bandsaw, your saw and your blade will last longer if you relax the tension when you are done for the day.

One last detail on blades: I have found that the length of coping saw blades isn't consistent. Some blades are longer than others. If your saw suddenly stops tensioning properly, it might be that your blades are a little too long.

HOW TO CUT

There is a lot of debate about whether you should set up the saw to cut on the pull or the push stroke. I think the answer is obvious: Orient the blade so the tearing or splintering from the blade is where you want it.

When your work is vertical in a vise or sawing donkey, the teeth should point away from the handle so the splintering is on the backside, which you cannot see while standing at the bench.

When sawing material held horizontally (more on that in a bit), orient the teeth so they point toward the handle. Then the splintering will be on the backside of the work facing the floor, which you cannot see while sawing.

Of course, if you are just removing dovetail waste with the saw, the tearing will be chopped away. So do whatever you like.

When you set up your work to saw it, many woodworkers prefer to saw the work while it's held vertically in a vise. And in some cases, such as when you are sawing dovetail waste, this is the best approach.

But when you look at 19th-century photos of schoolchildren sawing out a bird or squirrel shape, they're holding the work horizontally on a table

or a platform with a V-shaped cutout for support below (see the illustration below). With small pieces of work, you can hold the work with your off-hand and saw with your dominant hand, holding the saw vertical.

With big pieces of work, clamp the work to the bench (you can use your face vise or tail vise for outboard support) and hold the handle of the coping

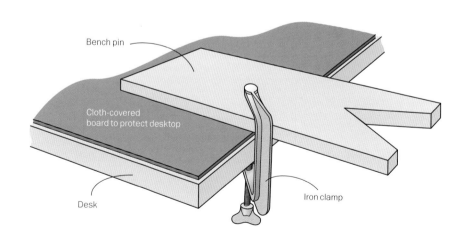

Bench pin

Cloth-covered board to protect desktop

Desk

Iron clamp

Cut anywhere. The V-shaped board, called a bench pin, acts as a sawing platform. With the blade cutting near the point of the V, thin materials won't vibrate during the cut.

COPING DOVETAIL WASTE IS AN OLD TECHNIQUE

I cope out the waste between my dovetails because that's how I learned to do it, and I am fast at it. When I demonstrate that technique, a common gripe from the peanut gallery is that it's an unnecessary modern complication to dovetailing.

It's actually not modern. In *Turning and Mechanical Manipulation* (1856), Charles Holtzapffel wrote:

"The wood between the dovetail pins is generally cut out with the bow or turning saw, leaving the space as at b, fig. 694; and the spaces are then pared out with the firmer chisel from opposite sides, as at c, the chisel being placed exactly on the gage lines, but slightly overhanging, so that the insides are cut hollow rather than square, to insure the exact contact at the inner and outer edges of the dovetails."

Unless you're a geologist, I consider 150-plus years to be a good long run for a woodworking technique.

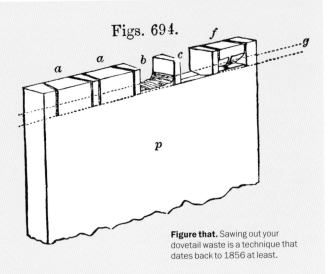

Figure that. Sawing out your dovetail waste is a technique that dates back to 1856 at least.

Sit and saw. When I cut scrollwork, I clamp the work flat on the bench and sit on a sawbench. Keep your chin right above the work and both hands on the saw if possible.

saw with both hands. Try it, and I think you will be shocked how easy it is to follow a line and keep your cut square to the face. Gravity is lending a hand.

When you saw with the work horizontal, try not to get too aggressive. You should feel like you are moving smoothly—not quickly—through the work. Speed will come in time with this method because gravity helps pull the saw down and into the cut, and it helps clear the kerf of dust as well.

Like with most things in handwork, it's more about finesse than force. And practice always helps. But there are times when the tool really is the culprit, and I'm afraid that is definitely the case with many coping saws. So fix your saw and learn to cope.

DISCOVER FLUSH-CUT SAW TECHNIQUES

Trim the fat from flush-cut saw techniques; with proper practice, your finished cuts will be extra-smooth.

BY GLEN D. HUEY

Bad technique or a bad saw? Either way, this is not good. The only recourse from here is to level the surface to the gash left by the saw.

This cut started on the right. Rolling the wrist caused the blade to ride upward as the cut progressed, which resulted in a higher left side. Additional work is needed to flush the peg. Holding the wrist level results in a smooth cut.

When I began building furniture, I bought a flush-cut saw. Knowing that I was going to build Shaker-style furniture and that square pegs were used in nearly every project, I was certain the saw would be one of the most-used hand tools in my shop. With saw in hand, and willing to spend some time testing the cut, I loaded a few pegs into a chunk of wood and started at it.

Having no formal woodworking education—I'd last received lessons in junior high shop class—I wasn't sure how to correctly handle the saw or even if I had my hands in the right position. Was there a proper method to using these saws? Pictures of the saws in woodworking catalogs show the blade of the saw bent just short of a 90° angle. I always wondered if this was the correct sawing position.

I positioned the saw flat to the surface while I sawed back and forth, allowing the saw blade to slide over the surface of the wood. Some cuts were acceptable, some weren't. Eventually I found more cuts weren't acceptable. The blade dug into the wood and my overall sanding time escalated as I found myself leveling the surface to remove the gash left in the wood. The saw was causing too much repair work. And so I pitched it into the garbage. Was I doing something wrong? Was my technique bad?

I then adopted a new technique of cutting close to the face of my project with a regular backsaw, then sanding the pegs flush with a random-orbit sander. Sometimes I'd place a piece of laminate or a business card over the peg and trim as close as possible then sand everything flush. I worked this way for years.

Recently, I brought a number of flush-cut saws into the shop to test and give it another chance. I loaded some pegs into a block of wood in order to per-form a couple dozen cuts and complete the tests.

Seeing the momentous number of advertisements and pictures of these saws being used with that huge bend, I again wondered if I was approaching this cut in the correct manner. Not wanting to miss an opportunity to learn, I bent the saw to that extreme angle and began to cut. Once again, it wasn't a good thing. At that angle, the saw cut worse than if I'd just taken a small hatchet and chopped at the peg. I couldn't keep the saw flat on the surface and the cut was ragged at best.

Practicing a few times with the same results, I began to think that I just wasn't going to be capable of using this technique to cut flush. So, I enlisted the help of editors Christopher Schwarz and Robert W. Lang to help uncover my problem. Was it me or were all those photos and advertisements wrong?

"Trust your gut instinct." "Your first thought is probably correct." Do these sayings sound familiar? They do to me. I contemplated these truisms as I watched Chris and Bob step to the bench one at a time. I didn't let them know what I was looking to find, only that I needed them to cut the peg with a flush-cut saw.

Much to my relief, they both approached the peg with the saw flat on the work and didn't bend the blade as they worked. I now knew the basic technique. What I needed was to refine the procedure and make the saws work for me instead of against me with that huge gash in the wood.

THE BASIC TECHNIQUE

I needed to start at the beginning, so I mulled over the process of using the flush-cut saw. First things first: Position the blade flat on the surface of the project. There shouldn't be any set in the teeth of a flush-cut saw, so placing the saw to either side of the peg is acceptable. I'm right-handed, thus you might think it's correct to begin with the blade on the right-hand side of the peg. However, if you're right-handed it's best if you begin with the saw on the left side of the peg. This requires that you rotate your wrist 180° or change your grip on the handle.

As we determine the correct placement of the left hand, you'll see why this saw positioning is so important. Two fingers of the left hand should hold the blade flat to the surface. This keeps the blade flat, minimizing the chance of it lifting from the surface, which would result in a proud peg. And, it prevents the teeth from diving into your nearly finished surface and causing those nasty gash lines.

Your fingers act as a hold-down for the saw as you stroke the saw back and forth, allowing the blade to slide between your fingers and the surface. Make sure that you hold your wrist so the blade remains flat. If you twist forward, you place additional stress at the front of the blade, which increases the chances of digging into the surface. If you twist back, you'll place that stress at the rear of the blade and your cut won't be flat and smooth across the peg. Using a saw with a wide blade provides a better chance to remain flat to the surface. A wide blade helps obtain a better cut.

And here is the importance of setting your hands properly: As you finish the cut through the peg, the saw blade isn't traveling toward your hand. If you've cut with your hands positioned differently—moving the blade toward your stationary hand—when you finished the cut I'll bet you jabbed the blade into your hand. I've seen this happen on more than one occasion in the classes I've taught. I'll let you in on a secret: I've done this a time or two myself. If you haven't made this mistake, consider yourself lucky, as well as warned.

Ideal hand placement. My fingers keep the blade flat on the surface. Once the cut is finished, the hand is clear of danger.

This cut is wrong in so many ways. The blade is not held flat, it's not supported through the cut, and the blade has direct access to the stationary hand. This is an accident waiting to happen.

LOCATION DICTATES THE DIRECTION

What happens when you need to make a cut with the blade positioned on the right-hand side of the peg because there isn't enough room on the left side of the peg for you to place the blade flat on the project?

If you're a left-handed woodworker, the procedure is as previously described, only mirrored. If you're a right-handed woodworker, the process requires a repositioning of the stationary (or left) hand.

Now, in order to keep your stationary hand out of the line of fire as you

Cutting toward your stationary hand. Make sure to raise the wrist and other appendages out of harm's way. Maintain two fingers on the blade for support and guidance.

Best teeth per inch (TPI). TPI influences the time required to make the cut. More teeth keeps the saw at its job longer, and that increases the chances for mistakes.

complete the cut, it's necessary to reach across the peg to place your fingers on the blade. (See the photo at top.) This position may feel awkward but, rest assured, you will not cut your hand as the saw slices through the peg.

MAKING THE FLUSH CUT

Hand positioning is covered—now, how do you cut? I've seen people try to make this cut using surprising techniques. One such technique was to slice through the cut by starting at the back

end of the blade and zipping completely past the front end of the blade—all in one swift motion. This action was repeated numerous times until the cut was complete—each time introducing the blade to the peg and the surface of the project.

Basic handsawing techniques suggest that you start the cut with a few short strokes in the direction that is opposite of the tool's cutting motion. On Western saws this would indicate a cut on the pull stroke. On the Japanese design, which includes most flush-cut saws, the cut would begin with a push stroke. Once the cut is begun and the saw is nestled into the kerf and running smooth, you should use full and complete strokes of the blade.

Using the entire blade does two things. First, it allows for better waste removal. When the gullets between the teeth fill up with dust, the saw stops cutting. Using full strokes helps empty the gullets. Second, using full strokes allows all the teeth to cut, which keeps the blade sharper longer. If you only use a small sampling of the teeth, those teeth wear faster.

One area of particular interest when using handsaws, especially thin-bladed saws such as the flush-cut saw, is the amount of pressure you exert as you saw. In working with any saw, the more force you use, the more apt you are to veer from the line. This happens (in part) because the blade bends or warps under the force.

Continuous sawing as the blade bends causes the kerf to drift. This is not acceptable when using the flush-cut saw. If your blade moves off the flat surface, you'll end up with a cut into the project or a cut that is nowhere near flush. In extreme instances, it's possible to actually kink the blade of flush-cut saws.

Allow the blade to cut with minimal pressure. If the length of time it takes to

Avoid ripping grain. Starting the cut on one side and finishing on the opposing side reduces any chances of ripping the grain down the side of the peg. A faux pas such as this shows in a finished project.

Clean out the glue. The main use for flush-cut saws in my woodworking is to trim pegs. Those often have been glued into position. The glue fills the teeth, rendering the saw useless. So you must clean the teeth well on a regular basis.

make the cut seems long, it's probably because the saw isn't sharpened correctly or the teeth per inch (TPI) count is high. The higher the TPI, the finer the cut—and the slower the cut is made. Lower TPI saws are more aggressive.

REFINING THE CUT

Should you perform the cut from only one direction, or do you start the cut on one side of a peg and then move to the second or opposing side to complete the operation?

The simplest method is to start the cut and saw through the entire peg. That's fine if all you're looking to do is hack away waste material. Much of the time, this is exactly what you're after. But problems surface if you catch the second-to-last stroke wrong. As you return to make the last stroke, it's possible to break the remaining material before it's cut by the teeth. Because the break is at the outer edge of the peg, it's conceivable that the fibers of the wood will tear down the peg side versus simply breaking off. That can leave a jagged finish to the peg that will require additional work or a nasty visible area that has to be addressed. This is the same reason why tree loggers make a relief cut on the back side of the trunk as they fell trees.

Creating a cut on one side prior to completing the cut from the opposing side reduces this possibility. If something does happen (say the peg breaks as the two cut areas intersect), the peg will not rip down the outer edge, but break somewhere in the interior of the peg. If material is left protruding from the surface, it's much easier to pare the center of the peg with a chisel without damaging the project surrounding the peg.

A FINAL NOTE

In most woodworking, if you're trimming pegs, chances are you've installed them using some type of glue. Glue is the enemy of flush-cut saws (and saws in general). The teeth are small and the glue easily becomes lodged in them. Within a short time, the saw becomes useless or untrustworthy as it cuts. Either scenario is something to avoid. Make sure to clean any glue remnants as soon as they're discovered.

Develop correct cutting methods and a flush-cut saw will reap huge rewards in your woodworking. These fine-toothed saws are indeed delicate, but, if cared for properly, they're capable of lasting a lifetime.

ACCESSORIES & PROJECTS

Put those skills to use. This section is full of projects to complement your newfound saw collection. The bench hook, sawbenches, and saw horses are must-have projects for increasing the utility of handsaws. The saw vise accessory will make filing and sharpening sawplates a snap, and you'll wonder how you ever measured panels before without the handy panel gauge. A convenient handsaw cabinet will house your collection. Finally, saw up a traditional six-board bench to display your handsaw skills.

THE BASIC BENCH HOOK

Three pieces of wood make crosscutting and planing easier—no matter where you work.

BY DON MCCONNELL

It's difficult to imagine the wooden bench hook without its almost constant companion, the backsaw. Indeed, this association is so strong that an alternative name for this useful hand-tool appliance is "saw rest."

For lighter sawing in the shop, the bench hook excels in effectiveness and convenience. The lower extension, or stop, "hooks" against the edge of the bench, and the material being sawn is held against the upper stop, as shown in the photo below. Because Western saws cut on the push stroke, the thrust of the saw helps hold the material in place. As a result, the bench hook and the material can be moved around at will, without any need for clamping or fastening.

Typically, the bench hook has a notch at the end of the upper stop (or a kerf is sawn into the stop) to allow the material to be fully supported while it is being cut. This arrangement also protects the benchtop from being damaged as the saw blade breaks through the work. The notch (or kerf) is located to the right of the stop for right-handers and to the left for left-handers.

The squared end of the stop can serve as a guide for the saw. For example, with the addition of a secondary "length stop" (which can be as simple as a strategically placed handscrew clamp), you can make repeated cuts of uniform length by using the squared end of the stop as a guide. This is a safe and effec-

tive way to cut short lengths of dowel stock, as shown on page 100.

However, I tend not to use the end of the stop as a saw guide. Rather, I work to knife lines on the material itself and use the notch as a "safe" area where saw cuts can be made without damaging the stop or the saw.

BUILDING A BENCH HOOK

As with all shop-made appliances, bench hooks can be constructed in any number of ways, depending on their intended usage and available materials.

The simplest, and possibly earliest, type of bench hook can be cut from a single piece of 4/4 material by drawing the shape of the two stops and the bed on the face grain and sawing them out. The hook will be quite narrow (the 1" thickness of the stock it was cut from) and you will need a pair of them to adequately support your work. Although this type of bench hook doesn't provide the same protection for the benchtop when cutting and isn't as adaptable, it is compact and portable.

The bench hook most commonly encountered today is constructed using three pieces of wood—a main bed piece of some length and width (10"-12" long and 7"-8" wide, typically), and two narrow projections, also known as "stops." These pieces are attached in various ways to the bed of the bench hook, depending on circumstances, available materials, and intended use.

Because bench hooks are often used in a somewhat sacrificial manner, they often are made without regard for the long-term effects of cross-grain construction. Indeed, a perfectly usable bench hook can be temporarily constructed simply by nailing the stops to the bed piece. A more common method is to affix the stops to the bed using glue and wooden pegs. If it isn't too wide and the bench hook isn't subjected to extreme environmental changes, a

A versatile item. Bench hooks can be used almost anywhere (such as on the bed of this jointer) and can do some surprising tasks. Here it is being used as a small planing board. The light-colored scrap below the work raises the work above the bench hook's stop.

BASIC BENCH HOOK CONSTRUCTION

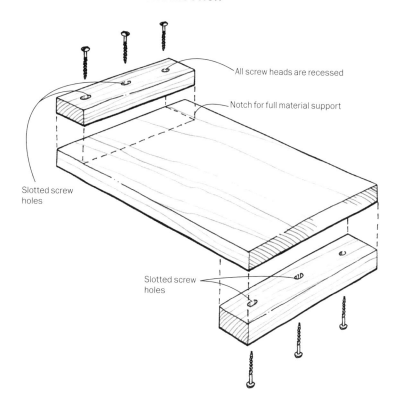

All screw heads are recessed

Notch for full material support

Slotted screw holes

Slotted screw holes

hook made this way will remain viable for a long time.

If you have suitable material and want a wider bed piece for your bench hook, it is possible to use slotted screw hole construction to attach the stops, as shown in the illustration on page 99. The actual construction method can vary, but it is best to recess the screw heads to eliminate the possibility of running the teeth of your saw into them. The location of the fixed screw on the upper stop isn't important, but it can be critical on the lower stop if you are planning to use the bench hook as a shooting board and need the end of the stop to remain flush with the edge of the bed. This form of construction is secure enough for most uses, while the slotted holes for the screws allow for the cross-grain movement of the wider bed piece.

MITER BLOCK FOR PRECISION SAWING

Though usually treated as a separate subject, the miter block can be seen as a specialized form of bench hook. This has both square and miter kerfs sawn into one of the stops that serve as effective guides for a backsaw.

Each kerf can be made with the aid of an accurately placed guide block, being sure to use the saw (preferably with minimal set) that will be in service for the subsequent work. When kerfs are made in a stop in this manner, it's desirable to glue the stop into a shallow rabbet in the end of the bed. This allows the stop to retain its lengthwise dimensional stability, and the integrity of the kerfs, despite the cross-grain construction.

The miter block is a useful alternative to a miter box when working with small pieces. If maintained and used with care, it is capable of precise work because it fully supports the material being sawn and the location of the cut can be precisely predicted. Its utility is

Cutting small pieces. Cutting short pieces to accurate length is a tricky operation with a miter saw. The bench hook, backsaw, and a handscrew clamp make the job safe and efficient.

MITER BLOCK

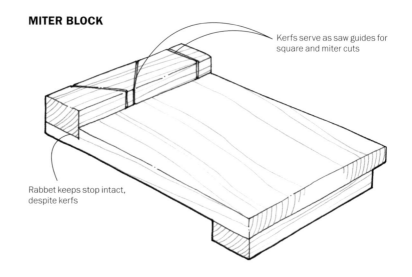

especially apparent with short pieces, which can be difficult or dangerous when being cut with a power miter saw.

Particularly when making miter cuts, it's often best to quickly secure the lower stop of the miter block in your bench vise to keep it from sliding sideways during use.

BENCH HOOKS AND PLANING

As already mentioned, a bench hook can be used in conjunction with a hand plane. For example, it can be turned over lengthwise so that the full length stop is at the top. In this orientation, it serves as a short shooting board to true the ends of smaller pieces. Sometimes it's desirable to place a thin scrap below the plane for it to run on, which protects the plane and adjusts its height so the cut takes place near the center of the iron.

Also, if you add a secondary "bed" that is slightly thinner than the stop, the bench hook can be used to plane thin stock of short lengths. Most of the time, this secondary bed can simply lie on the main bed with its end against the stop. In this usage, the bench hook serves as a small planing board.

The versatility of the bench hook also makes it a prime candidate for

Shooting board. The bench hook makes an effective shooting board for truing the ends of small pieces. The piece of scrap below the plane protects the side of the tool and centers the tool's cutter on the work.

various kinds of on-site work. As long as there is a surface to place the bench hook on, plus an edge that you can rest the lower stop against, it can be used for all of the above-mentioned functions— all while protecting the saw or plane and the surface on which the bench hook rests. I've used bench hooks on the top tread of a staircase, the edge of a porch, and on the tops of table saws and jointers.

Especially for shorter, thinner, narrower or awkward pieces, a bench hook and backsaw can provide a safe and versatile option for any woodworker, either at the bench or out on the work site.

BENCH HOOK HISTORY

Some readers might be surprised to learn that Joseph Moxon, in his *Mechanick Exercises or the Doctrine of Handy-Works* (published serially between 1678 and 1680), uses the term "bench hook" to describe a device we know today as a bench stop or a bench dog. In other words, it is a device that is installed in a recess in the benchtop, that projects just above the surface and that prevents material from moving forward while being planed. The type of "bench hook" illustrated by Moxon has a lateral projection at its upper end that gives it the appearance of a hook. This usage is largely obsolete now, though it continued until at least the middle of the 19th century.

Because the wooden shop appliance we now know as the bench hook is closely associated with backsaws, it is tempting to hypothesize that it arose as a common shop accessory in conjunction with the emergence of backsaws. Because backsaws first appeared about Moxon's time, it seems likely that the wooden bench hook first emerged not long after. However, the first illustration of a wooden bench hook that I'm aware of isn't until in Peter Nicholson's *Mechanical Exercises*, published in 1812.

SAWBENCH & SHOP STOOL

This simple afternoon project is perfect for handsawing, holding doors for planing, organizing tools, and giving you a leg up.

BY JOHN WILSON

My simple plywood two-step in the old tool shed had reached the end of the road. Looking at it, you could see a pile of old wood ready for the burn pile. What I saw in it was a project that recalled 45 years of working life. It was more than just memories that came to mind. If it was time to recycle the old stool, then it was important to document what had been a most useful object, and perhaps make a successor to it before its last rites.

My time in home building and remodeling went back to four summers during college. I learned the trade of carpentering before the modern era of specialization, the days when a small carpenter crew did everything from the first framing to a completed house ready for painters. It was a good education. The shop stool represented a sort of rite of passage into the world of construction.

That first summer I was too busy learning the ropes as the new kid to understand the significance of a shop stool. I borrowed someone else's when a task was at ceiling height. The second summer I was more confident of what was required on the job. After all, they had hired me back.

One day the boss suggested I stop by his shop to make a shop stool. It sounded helpful to me, but looking back on it

EXPLODED VIEW

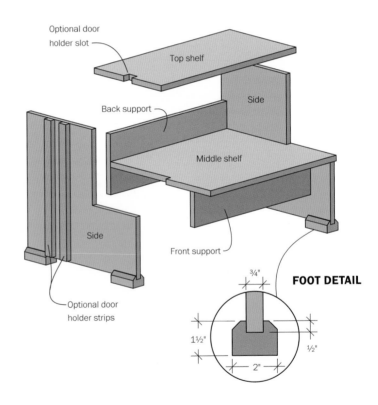

Optional door holder slot

Top shelf

Back support

Side

Side

Middle shelf

Front support

Optional door holder strips

FOOT DETAIL

3/4"

1½"

½"

2"

Construction steps:

1. After cutting all the plywood pieces (see page 104), round over all the exposed edges in the stool using a ⅛"-diameter roundover router bit.
2. Assemble pieces using tapered drill and countersink to drill for 1⅝" deck screws. Start with the front and back supports on the middle shelf.
3. Cut 4"-long hardwood blocks for the feet with a groove to fit ¾" plywood. Adjust the thickness of the blocks to make the stool level and glue them in place.
4. Finish with a sealer coat of polyurethane and thinner mixed 50/50.

from the perspective of years later I can see its significance. It marked my acceptance as a man who could use an on-site bench to do his work. From now on, along with my growing box of tools, the back of my car held my very own work stool, something some newer member of the crew would ask to borrow. That pile of old plywood ready for the burn pile was to me a badge of rank, hard won during months of work on the job.

So what was so special about the shop stool on the job? The place at which you work is an important extension of the tools you use. This is as true of home building and remodeling as it is in the workshop. In fact, this shop stool is an asset in either your shop or on the building site.

■ It serves as a stable two-step work platform.

■ It's a mobile work surface for cutting and assembly.

■ It securely holds doors on edge for planing tasks.

■ Two stools will replace the need for sawhorses.

■ It keeps tools in one place where they are easier to find and transport to a new work site.

All of this is from a half sheet of ¾" plywood and some deck screws. Recalling all the ways the shop stool gives good service made me realize how important it was to record its dimensions. I inherited mine from men of experience on the job. There is no better school of design than experience. So here it is for you, too.

CONSTRUCTION TIPS

While plywood is a stock construction item, I found that its quality varied considerably and that taking time to shop for a good sheet paid off. Look for a piece with reasonable finish, free from major voids, and not warped. Some of the best plywood is made of yellow pine; look for BC grade with one good face. Pick the best you can.

The illustrations and cutting plan give you direction. Start by screwing the 8" back support to the middle shelf, and then screw the 5" front support under the middle shelf, leaving it centered with ⅞" exposed at each end. With these in place, the sides will screw to the middle shelf more easily. The top step goes on and you are done. It's that simple.

The door holder slot, if desired, is added to one side. And there is one more addition that will add years of life to your shop stool. I found that the plywood feet abraded away with use, as you can see in the picture below. As that happens, the stool loses stability as well. So I made some simple hardwood blocks. The blocks are made from a piece of 1 ½" x 2" with a groove ¾" wide by ½" deep routed into the wider face. Cut these into four pieces 4" long and glue them onto the sides.

One further use of the stool comes at noon—all the guys sitting around the work site with their lunch pails open!

CUTTING PLAN

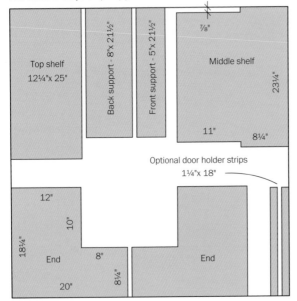

Half sheet ¾" BC yellow pine plywood

Top shelf
12¼"x 25"

Back support - 8"x 21½"

Front support - 5"x 21½"

⅞"

Middle shelf

23¾"

11"

8¼"

Optional door holder strips
1¼"x 18"

12"

10"

18¼"

End

8"

8¼"

End

20"

The original stool. Here is the old stool after a life of usefulness, now on the burn pile to be returned to basic elements of the universe and to be recombined into a new generation of materials. Note the badly worn corners where the plywood feet gave out. The attachment of the hardwood "shoes" as I describe will extend the life of your stool.

TRADITIONAL SAWBENCH

Once you build a sawbench, you will wonder how you ever worked wood without it.

BY CHRISTOPHER SCHWARZ

Versatile and sturdy. The reason sawbenches are so useful is the top. The fact that it is flat and has some width allows you to perform many operations on it. And the particular height of the sawbench unleashes the effectiveness of full-size Western-style handsaws and panel saws.

Sawbenches are not sawhorses. Though both devices support your work, real sawbenches can be pressed to do so much more that they are worth building in a long afternoon in the shop.

The major difference between a sawbench and a sawhorse is the top. On a sawhorse, the top is generally long and skinny. It will not support anything on its own. A sawbench has a wide top: 7" is a common and useful width. And it's this detail alone that makes them worth building. The wide top allows you to cut many cabinet-sized parts using one sawbench alone. The top is also an excellent clamping surface, allowing you to secure work to it. The sawbench is a step stool for reaching up high. It's a mortising stool for hand-mortising operations—you secure the work over a leg and hold it down with a holdfast (hence the hole in the top). And then you sit on the sawbench astride or next to your work.

But, as they say on television, there's more. Much more. The shelf below holds your square and saw as you move your stock in position. The V-shaped mouth on the top—called a "ripping notch"—supports your work as you notch out corners with a handsaw or jigsaw. And the top is the traditional place for a craftsman to sit when eating lunch.

The sawbench shown here is based entirely on traditional English forms. If you choose to alter this plan, resist changing the height of the sawbench. The 20" height is key to using the bench in conjunction with a Western handsaw. The 20" height allows you to use your legs to secure your work without clamps and makes the handsaw work efficiently. The sawbench is high enough that a 26"-long saw at the proper cutting angle won't hit the floor and the saw won't be able to jump out of its kerf on the return stroke.

END VIEW

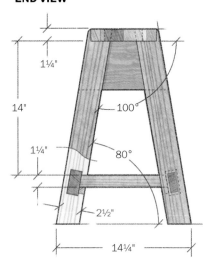

LEG JOINT DETAIL

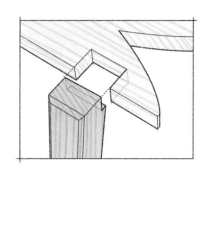

TOP VIEW

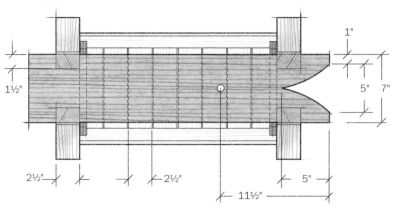

CUT LIST & MATERIALS

NO.	ITEM	DIMENSIONS (INCHES)			MATERIAL	COMMENTS
		T	W	L		
☐ 1	Top	1¼	7	32	Pine	
☐ 4	Legs	2½	2½	21	Pine	Includes extra length for trimming
☐ 2	Lower braces	1¼	2½	26¼	Pine	2⅝"-long tenon, both ends
☐ 2	Shelf braces	¾	⅝	21	Pine	10° bevel on one long edge
☐ 8	Shelf pieces	1¼	2½	9¼	Pine	10° bevel on both ends, cut to fit
☐ 2	Top braces	¾	5	9½	Plywood	10° angle on edges, cut to fit

Build your sawbench out of any material that is plentiful, inexpensive, and easy to work. The legs and lower braces are assembled as follows: Create the through-mortise by cutting away the material before gluing the two pieces together that form each leg. If you like, chamfer all the edges of your components with a block plane or chamfer bit in a router.

Cut the ends of the legs at 10°, then cut a notch at the top of each leg that will allow it to nest into notches in the top piece. Each leg notch measures ½" x 2½" x 1¼". Cut your tenons on the lower braces, then assemble the braces and legs. Drawbore the joints, then wedge them using hardwood wedges and glue.

With the legs and braces assembled, clamp them temporarily to the top and mark precisely where they intersect the edges of the top. Take the clamps off and mark out the 1½" x 2½" notches in the top that will receive the legs. Saw out the notches and cut the ripping notch. Glue the leg assemblies to the top and reinforce the joint with a ½"-diameter dowel.

Clamp the plywood top braces in place and trace the angle of the legs on the braces. Unclamp the braces and saw each one to shape. Glue and screw the braces to the legs using three #8 x 2" wood screws in each leg. If you want to add a shelf, first rip a 10° bevel on the

FRONT VIEW

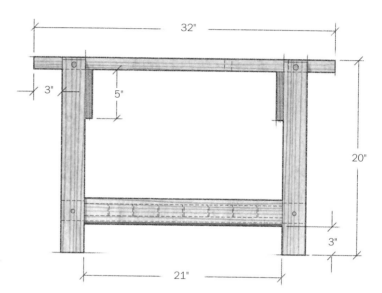

shelf braces and cut the ends of the shelf pieces at 10°. With the sawbench upside down on your bench, place the shelf pieces against the lower braces. Glue the shelf braces against the shelf pieces and nail everything in place.

Bore a ¾"-diameter hole in the top for a holdfast or hold-down. Position the hole so the pad of the holdfast will touch the tops of the legs. Mine is positioned to accommodate a specific hold-down.

BREAKDOWN SAWHORSES

Practice your hand-tool skills and make a pair of strong, collapsible workshop companions.

BY WILL MYERS

There are many designs out there for different styles of knock-down or fold-up sawhorses; a lot of them are very good and would serve the purpose perfectly. The biggest problems with most designs is that their construction tends to get complicated and heavy. It is just a sawhorse; should it really take a month to make two?

This design is the culmination of things my previous sawhorses lacked. I wanted a sawhorse that was relatively lightweight (could be moved one handed); could be broken down or assembled simply and quickly; could lie flat for storage or transport; didn't need tools other than a hammer or mallet; and most of all, strong with no wiggle.

MATERIALS

These sawhorses are made from yellow pine construction lumber. I find it worthwhile to pick through the pile to find quartersawn stock, but flat-sawn stock will do just fine. If yellow pine is unavailable, use whatever cheap and relatively strong species you can get. I picked up two 16' 2 x 10s to build these two sawhorses and had a good bit left.

Choose lumber wisely. It's worth digging to find quartersawn yellow pine—it's a perfect material for sawhorses.

Square your stock. A powered jointer makes for fast work flattening stock.

Glue it up. A small foam roller works well for spreading the glue evenly and quickly.

One more thing to consider is the moisture content of construction lumber. Straight from the home center, it tends to be a bit on the wet side. Let it acclimate for a little while and dry out before you start to mill it.

BEAM GLUE-UP

I usually build these in pairs; one sawhorse is about as useful as a water hose with no spigot. Mill out the stock for the beams first; you will need four pieces about 3¾" x 36". This is slightly larger

Clamp the beams together. Clamp both beams at once. I also have a scrap piece on the outside of the stack to prevent the clamps from damaging the beam surfaces.

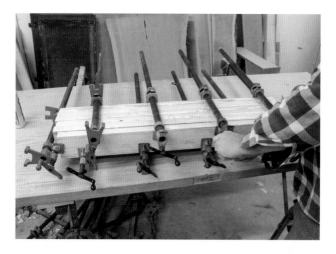

than final size and will be milled to final specs after glue-up.

We want to keep the beams as thick as possible. Because we are starting with 1½"-thick stock, joint just one face of each of the four pieces that will meet when glued, taking just enough material off to get a flat surface. Align the pieces and draw a triangle on one pair and two triangles on the second, so as you are gluing you will know which pieces go together. Apply glue to the meeting faces of each pair, assemble, and clamp the two beam assemblies as one. While the glue sets, you can get the legs started.

CUT THE LEG ASSEMBLIES

The plans for these sawhorses call for a total height of 30"—you can, of course, make them taller or shorter to suit your needs. You will need eight legs for two sawhorses. These are jointed and planed to 1⅜" x 3¼" x 32". (The 32" length is slightly over long—you'll cut them to size later). Arrange the legs in pairs and mark the faces; it is a good idea to number the pairs as well. Start by cutting the tops of the legs at a 15° angle.

Clamp a pair of legs together with the inside edges up then measure down from the top 5½" and square a line across both legs.

Unclamp the legs. On the face side of the leg, place a try square on the angled top of the leg, line up the beam of the square to the line you just made on the side, and pencil a mark to the top of the leg. This will be the meeting face between the legs.

Now, measure over from the line on the face ¾" toward the outside of the leg and make a tick mark. Use a machinist square with the rule set to project 3½" from the fence. Line the square up to the tick mark; pencil a mark down the rule and around the end. This notch will become the saddle that the top beam will rest in.

With the layout on the ends of the legs complete, it's time to rip! Start by ripping the 3½" line first down to the baseline; make a crosscut at the baseline of the saddle to remove the waste.

With the saw cuts complete, check for square. If the notch needs any tuning, a chisel will make quick work of it. The lower angle needs to be flat and square; a block plane works well here.

STRETCHER MORTISE AND TENONS

For the stretchers that run between the legs, you will need four ⅞" x 2" x 18" pieces of stock. These keep the bottoms

Lay out both legs together. Laying out the legs in pairs ensures perfect alignment.

Add the angle. Square off of the 15° cut at the top of the leg.

SAWHORSE ASSEMBLY

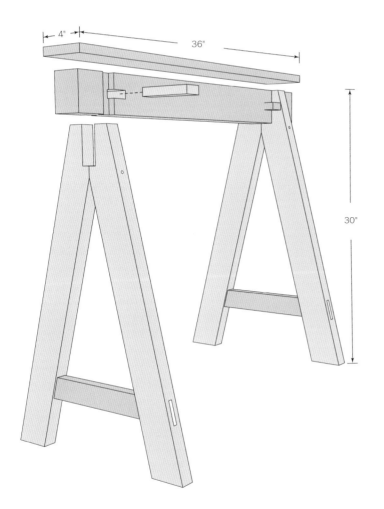

Two-part layout. You can lay out the side and bottom of the saddle notch at once.

Cut the angle. A full-size rip saw makes quick work of cutting these angles.

A crucial cut. This short rip cut needs to be accurate; the top of the legs attach to one another here.

CUT LIST & MATERIALS

NO.	ITEM	DIMENSIONS (INCHES)			MATERIAL	NOTES
		T	W	L		
☐ 1	Top cap	¾	4½	36	Pine	
☐ 1	Beam	3½	2¾	35	Pine	
☐ 4	Legs	1⅜	3¼	32	Pine	Trimmed to length.*
☐ 2	Stretchers	⅞	2	18	Pine	
☐ 2	Wedges	¾	1¾	6	White oak	

*Give yourself extra length here. The legs are best cut to final length after assembly.

Direct layout. Transferring the stretcher mortise locations to the legs using the stretcher itself is the most accurate method.

the top meeting surfaces of the legs and use a clamp to hold them in alignment.

Lay the stretcher on top of the legs with the line you just made aligned with the top edge. Hold the stretcher in place and trace with a pencil around the upper and lower sides of the stretcher onto the faces of the legs. Before removing the stretcher, also trace from the inside of the legs to the underside of the stretcher for the tenon shoulder location. Laying out the joints this way assures perfect alignment even though both elements of the joints are angled.

I usually cut the tenons first. Line up a bevel to the trace mark on the face of the stretcher and knife the shoulder line in. Use a square to knife the line across the edges, and finish by knifing the shoulder on the opposite face with the bevel. To lay out the thickness of the tenon, use a mortise gauge set to ⅜".

Center the gauge teeth to the thickness of the stretcher, with the fence to the face side; gauge around the sides and end of the tenon. Then, saw a kerf for tenon wedges ¼" from the top and bottom edges of the tenons.

For the mortise layout, transfer the marks made earlier across the edges of the legs with a square. The leg is thicker than the stretcher, so you will need to

of the legs from spreading when under heavy load. To lay out the mortise and tenons, start by clamping the pair of legs to be joined in the vise with the outside edge up and the top angles aligned with one another. Measure down 22½" from the top of the leg and square a line across the two. Remove the legs from the vise and lay them out flat on the bench with the face side up. Align

Tenon width. Set your gauge teeth to the width of your mortise chisel.

Gauge the mortise. Gauge the mortise width between the pencil marks on the insides and outsides off the legs.

Lay out the shoulders. A crosscut-filed backsaw takes care of the shoulder cuts.

readjust the fence on the gauge to center the teeth on the leg stock. Gauge the mortise width between the pencil marks on the inside and outside edges of the legs.

Chop out the waste, working halfway from either side, meeting in the middle. The ends of the mortise are at an angle; as you are chopping, you can eyeball down the back of the chisel to the layout lines down the side of the legs to help get an accurate angle through the mortise.

With the mortises complete, dry fit the assembly. Check that the tenon shoulders fit to the insides of the legs; use a chisel or shoulder plane to pare away any offending material. The tenons will need to be cut to length. While assembled, trace the length from the side of the legs onto the tenon. Also check the tops of the legs where they meet one another; this area can be tuned with a block plane or sawn while assembled with a tenon saw to close up the joint.

The area at the top of the legs where they meet will be secured by a single #14 x 4" wood screw (a hexhead lag bolt could be substituted here). While dry fitted, use a bevel set at 15° and make a reference line through the middle of the

OPTIONAL LEG ASSEMBLY METHOD

Another version of leg assembly that works well involves nails instead of mortise-and-tenon joints. In this version, the legs are made the same as described; the difference is that a short upper stretcher is attached with nails and glue to the side of the legs at the top, replacing the screw. The lower stretcher is also just nailed in place, eliminating the mortise-and-tenon joints. While the nailed leg assemblies are not as elegant a solution to joining the legs together, it is much faster to build and plenty strong.

pad on the face of the legs where they meet; then, square the line around the side of the leg. Clamp the legs together to hold them in alignment.

With a ½" auger centered on the leg, bore in to a depth of about 1¼" using the bevel line to sight the angle. Use a ¼" drill to bore through the center of the auger hole until it just starts into the adjoining leg.

Disassemble and finish by boring the adjoining leg for the threaded portion of the screw with a ³⁄₁₆" drill bit.

Before final assembly of the legs, there are a couple of tasks that are better done now than later. Finish plane all four sides of the stretcher. These sawhorses are meant to be used—they're not fine furniture—so I cut the chamfered edges with a jack plane, eyeballing a 45° angle. If the bevel is rough, make a final pass or two with the block plane. I also chamfer the inside edges of the legs that cannot be reached once assembled with a smoothing plane.

The legs also need to be cut to final length by measuring down from the top

Wedged tenons. A saw kerf ¼" or so from the top and bottom edges of the tenons will make starting the wedges easy.

30", then using the bevel to lay out the same 15° angle as the top. Saw the line; the legs will look like a parallelogram when laid out correctly. If it looks like a trapezoid it won't work!

Join the legs. Use a ¼" drill centered in the auger hole; stop drilling when it just starts in the opposite leg. Just the one screw is all that is needed to secure the tops of the legs together.

LEG ASSEMBLY

Spread a good coat of glue on the tenons, mortises, and the area at the top of the legs where they meet. Assemble the tenons with their respective mortises.

Align the tops of the legs, place a clamp across to hold the faces flush with one another, and install the screw.

Last, drive the wedges into the stretcher tenons. As you drive the wedges in, be sure the leg stays tight against the stretcher shoulders.

FINISH THE BEAMS

Once the glue is dry on the beams, joint and plane them to their final dimensions of 3½" x 2¾" x 35". There are four short dados that need to be cut into the beam that capture the legs. Measure in from both ends 4" and knife a line around all four sides.

Now measure in 1⅜" from the first line and square it around all four sides as well. Set a single pin gauge to ⅝" and on the top and bottom of the beam gauge a line between the two knife marks for the depth of the dados.

Cut the dado. Saw the sides of the dado first, down to the depth mark, then chop out the waste. Finish by paring down to the baseline.

Define the angle. Use the wedge to transfer the angle.

Mortise for the wedge. Lay out your angled mortise and then auger out most of the waste.

Check the fit and insert the leg assemblies in the dados. They should just slide in; a little loose is better than too tight.

WEDGES

Use as hard a wood as you can get your hands on for the wedges; I am using white oak for these shown. To make the wedges, start with a piece of wood ¾" x 1¾" x 6". The wedges are a little long at 6", but this gives some leeway for fitting, and they will be shortened later. Measure down ⅝" on the face of the wedge stock on one end and make a tick mark. Align a straightedge with the tick mark and the areas at the opposite end; mark down the length with a pencil.

It is a good idea that the wedges be identical to one another so that they will seat up the same in any mortise in which they're placed. To accomplish this, make the final passes with the jointer plane while all four wedges are aligned to one another and clamped up in the vise.

To lay out the mortises for the wedges, assemble the legs to the beam while they are upside down on the bench. Lay the wedge against the underside of the beam, straight side against the inside face of the legs. Make a pencil mark down the angled side of the wedge onto the beam. Disassemble and, using a square, bring the line up both sides. Gauge with the fence to the bottom side and mark from the pencil line to the dado. Using an auger slightly smaller than the width of the mortise, bore halfway through from both sides and then chop out the remaining waste with a ¾" chisel.

FINISHING UP

Finish-plane the sides and bottom of the beam. You can also chamfer the lower edges and end to match the legs if you like. Assemble the legs to the base and drive the wedges up tight. The wedges will also be extending past the legs a bit; mark where they meet the legs and saw off the extra length. Chamfering the ends of the wedges will help keep them from mushrooming as they are driven in and out. If the legs are projecting above the top of the beam, plane them flush or a shade below. Last but not least, nail (no glue) a ¾" x 4¼" x 36" board to the top of the beam to serve as a top cap.

I wiped a coat of oil on these for a finish, but no finish at all is just fine too.

A little extra room. Chop an extra ³⁄₁₆" into the dado. The wedge should push against the leg and not bottom out in the mortise.

Clean up with a plane. After the glue sets, saw the wedges off flush and plane the faces and outside edges to smooth and remove any layout and milling marks left behind.

SHOP-MADE SAW VISE

Combine wood, leather, and steel for a new take on an old tool.

BY JASON THIGPEN

If you sharpen your own handsaws, a proper saw vise is an essential tool. The jaws on a saw vise clamp down tightly on the sawplate, holding it securely as you file each tooth. A well-built saw vise will absorb vibration and chatter, resulting in faster filing, longer file life, and better results.

There are a handful of new vises in production today and vintage versions are plentiful. Vintage versions are great, but damage and wear can pose problems. The clamping mechanisms on a lot

Clamping mechanism ready for welding. I chuck the handles in my drill press and buff them to a sheen using progressively finer grits of sandpaper. After welding, I apply gun bluing.

Using a hacksaw, cut a 4 ½" length of threaded rod. Weld a nut on one end, creating the threaded post. For the wing nut, cut two 2 ¼"-long pieces of ½" rod. One end needs to be flat, while the other gets a bevel of around 25°. (I've found 25° is just the right angle to provide a solid grip while remaining low profile.) A simple wooden jig holds the components in place while they are welded together. Then apply a coat of gun bluing to the hardware, followed by a few coats of 3-in-1 oil. (Acme handle nuts can be pur-

chased if you wish to buy rather than make a handle.)

JAW PREP

I used a single piece of 8" x 18" 8/4 rift-sawn white oak for the jaws, ripping the piece in half after the following steps.

My longest backsaw is 16" long and my largest handsaw is 28" long. The 18" jaw length of the saw vise allows me to sharpen every backsaw I own without repositioning them. My handsaws only have to be repositioned once. Only the

of old vises are a weak spot, either broken or worn past the point of use.

After months of searching for a well-made unit that wouldn't require a lot of rehab, I began to design my own saw vise. The result is a vise that not only has a classic look—it is a workhorse that has greatly surpassed the performance of any other vise I've tried, new or old.

All you need to make it are a few off-the-shelf components and a weekend. You can use any hardwood you like, provided it's straight-grained, rift-sawn or quartersawn material. For this vise, I used some hard maple and white oak scraps.

CLAMPING MECHANISM

This shop-made saw vise excels due to a few key features that all work together. The heart of the system is the ⅝", eight threads-per-inch Acme-threaded screw and wing nut. Acme thread is capable of applying a great deal of force, and the threads won't gall, strip, or weaken over time.

I used this combination with great success on a Moxon vise I built during the past year. The wing-nut assembly can be easily made if you have access to a welder. If not, buddy up with a local welder and have him or her fabricate one for you. It's simple and straightforward.

Jaw recess. Hogging out the excess using a stacked dado set is the most efficient stock removal method to create the jaw's recess.

Cleaning time. I use a high-angle smoothing plane to clean up all of the jaw surfaces after rough shaping. The 60° tool works well on white oak, leaving behind a glassy surface.

Shape shifter. A custom template for your vise jaws allows you to play with a multitude of shapes and configurations. Find one that accommodates all of your saws while leaving mass in the center where it's needed.

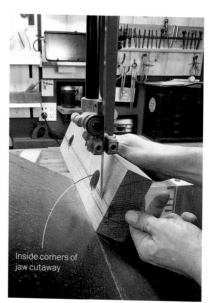

Inside corners of jaw cutaway

Less is more. Removing material on the outside of the jaws makes it easier to file, allowing you to add slope to your gullets if so desired.

Straight and square. After roughing out the stock and letting it acclimate, I check for twist using a set of winding sticks. I square the stock using handplanes before laying out the joinery.

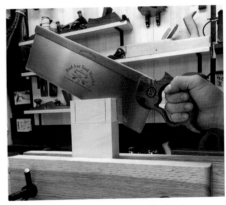

Moxon moxie. Using a Moxon-style vise to elevate the work, I cut the tenons by hand. (Use your excess Acme thread to make one of these devices; you won't regret it.)

CUT LIST & MATERIALS

NO.	ITEM	DIMENSIONS (INCHES)			MATERIAL	COMMENTS
		T	W	L		
☐ 2	Jaws	2	4	18	White oak	
☐ 1	Front leg	1½	4	21	Maple	TOE*
☐ 1	Back leg	1½	4	13	Maple	TOE*
☐ 1	Hinge	½	1	4	White oak	
☐ 1	Dowel	⅝-dia.	-	1	Hardwood	
☐ 1	Threaded rod	⅝-8	-	36	Acme	
☐ 2	Threaded nuts	⅝-8	-		Acme	
☐ 1	Extra-thick washer	⁵⁄₁₆	-			
☐ 1	Flat-head socket cap screw	¼-20		2¾ long		
☐ 1	Threaded insert	¼-20			Brass	
☐ 1	Rod	½-dia.	-	12	Steel	
☐ 1	Strip	-	1	50	Cowhide strip	
*TOE = Tenon one end						

EXPLODED VIEW

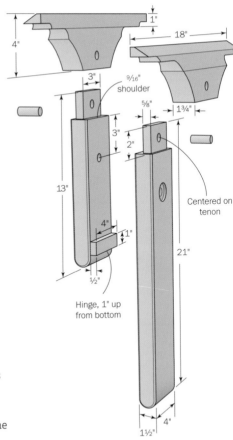

top 1" section of the jaws will contact the sawplate.

To accommodate the thicker back on a backsaw, cut a ¼"-deep recess in all but the top 1" of each jaw. This is best accomplished with a stacked dado set on the table saw.

With the fence set 1" from the blade, make your initial pass on the jaw, then rotate the workpiece and make a pass on the other long edge. Incrementally move

the fence away with each successive pass until the recess is complete.

Change to a rip blade, then rip the piece in half. You are left with two jaws that are 4" x 18", and each has a 1"-wide "grip" at the top.

The jaws are shaped to work with the saws in my arsenal. I prepared a template for the jaws using poster board, then placed each saw I own on it to simulate the actual filing position.

ADJUSTING THE VISE JAWS

When first setting up your saw vise, the jaws need to be adjusted for the whole assembly to work correctly. Ideally, any saw that is inserted into the vise will be held in place without pressure from the screw.

The ends of both jaws should make contact at all times. It is this contact that holds the saw in place while you fine-tune the position of the teeth. This is where the beauty of the leather-clad hinge is realized. The leather compresses, allowing you adjust the contact between the jaws by tightening or loosening the two screws.

Use an Allen wrench to slowly tighten each screw until the corresponding end of the hinge makes contact. There should still be a gap of at least 1⁄16" in the middle of both jaws; this will close up when the Acme screw is tightened.

If the contact between the jaws changes over time, use the screws to adjust it until it a saw can be supported.

Consistent alignment. Two Allen-head screws pass through the hinge assembly and screw into threaded brass inserts. I like to mark the orientation of my hinge; it helps keep the jaw alignment consistent if you have to disassemble and reassemble the vise.

No-headache tension. By tightening each screw, you can increase the tension on each end of the jaws' spring joint. Snug the screws down until a standard handsaw can be supported without any assistance from the wing nut. Adjust the hinge as needed for seasonal changes and wear.

I marked where the handles interfere with the vise jaws, then used those marks to dictate the shape of the jaws. Using a combination of drafting templates, I sketched out a shape that was both pleasing and functional. The tops and backsides of each jaw are angled so I can get up close with my saw files, adding slope to my gullets if needed.

Mark a 1⁄4" flat along the jaw face, then two bevels on the edges. Then mark and drill 1½"-diameter holes for the inside corners of the jaw cutaway. Rough out the chamfers on the bandsaw; clean up the cuts with handplanes.

The goal is to remove as much "visual" weight from the vise as possible while retaining its mass and strength where needed (similar to the concept behind Windsor chair seats).

Once the bevels are done, cut the jaws to shape at the bandsaw, then clean up the cuts using a combination of rasps, files, and scrapers.

LEG PREP

The legs are built from 6/4 hard maple and are cut to a final width of 4". I machine all of the components to almost final dimension a few weeks prior to the build to allow them to accli-

Plumb the depths. I hog out most of the mortise waste on the underside of the jaws using a 5⁄8" Forstner bit at the drill press, then use a wide chisel to clean up the edges and corners. The valleys created by the bit make a good guide to create plumb walls.

Nut housing. To house the nut on the threaded rod, chop out a mortise on the back of the rear leg. A 1" Forstner bit removes most of the waste; a chisel takes care of the rest.

mate to the shop. Then, using winding sticks and handplanes, I fine-tune each one before cutting the joinery. Square stock is vital to this build.

JOINERY PREP

To accommodate the massive force that can be applied by the Acme screw, I decided on a drawbored mortise-and-tenon joint between each leg and its corresponding jaw. The parts will be assembled later, but first cut the joinery and drill for the hardware

The leg tenons are ⅝" thick, 3" wide, and 2" long. I offset my tenons toward the outside, using a 9/16" interior shoulder to keep a flush surface on the inside of the jaws.

Flush the legs at the top, clamp them together, then mark and drill a pilot hole located on center 3" from the shoulder for alignment. On the front of the front leg, drill a shallow 1⅜"-diameter recess to house the washer.

On the inside surface of the back leg, drill a ⅝"-deep, 1"-diameter hole, then trim it with chisels to form a six-sided mortise to house the captured nut for the wing-nut assembly.

Drill ⅝"-diameter through-holes in each leg for the threaded Acme rod.

LEATHER HINGE

The jaws on a saw vise don't need to open up a lot to work effectively because most sawplates are less than .040" thick. A hinge that opens farther just adds potential for slop to be introduced.

By using a ½" x 1" x 4" "hinge" of white oak with leather strips glued to each side, the jaws can be opened enough to slip a saw in while introducing a clamping force that holds the saw in place, even with the Acme screw loose. This allows you to fine-tune the position of a saw before final tightening. This force can be adjusted using two hinge mounting screws (see "Adjusting the Vise Jaws" on page 119).

For those screws, drill two ¼" countersunk through-holes from the front of the long leg, located 9 ½" up from the bottom of the long leg and 1" in on each side. Now clamp the legs together with the inside faces touching, and mark the inside face of the short leg for the threaded-insert hole locations (1½" from the bottom of the leg).

Though the packaging says to use a ⅜" bit for the threaded-insert mortise, I prefer a 25/64" bit; the tolerances are too tight with the smaller bit.

Drill mortises and place the threaded inserts in them.

The last bit of drilling is for the two ¼" through-holes in the hinge (the leather won't hurt the bit).

COMPOUND SPRING JOINT

The final and most important feature of this saw vise is what I've dubbed a "compound spring joint." This is a spring joint on both the vertical and horizontal planes of the jaw. You're likely familiar with the concept of a spring joint when gluing panels; the concept works the same here. I like to add both spring joints as the final step in shaping the jaws. A lot of material has been removed from the jaws at this point, so some movement is to be expected.

Check the jaw faces for square and fine-tune as needed.

Use a block plane to create the vertical spring joint. Taper the jaw face inward by a few degrees, starting at the top and working down. When the Acme screw is tightened, the initial contact is at the top of the jaws. As you tighten, the legs will bow slightly inward, causing the jaws to ever-so-slightly pull in as well. That results in a solid 1" contact area along the length of the vise.

For the lateral spring joint, start in the middle of each jaw; take light passes and work your way to the ends. The final concavity should be right at 1/16" in the middle.

Depressing work. Using a block plane, start forming the lateral spring joint by taking a few light passes in the middle, working your way to the edges with each pass. The resulting depression should be approximately 1/16" when complete.

It is imperative that you don't alter the vertical spring joint while planing the lateral one.

In use, when the Acme screw is tightened and the spring joints close up, the resulting grip on the sawplate is amazing.

FINAL ASSEMBLY

Once the jaws have been shaped, spread a liberal layer of glue into the mortise, insert the tenon, and drive that ⅝" dowel home. The joint should be rock-solid and ready for a century or more of use.

After trimming and flushing the dowels, it's time to add the leather strips to the jaws and complete final shaping.

Gluing leather strips to each jaw face not only increases the grip strength, it also protects your saws from damage. Liquid hide glue and plastic wrap make quick work of the leather install.

After the glue sits overnight, remove the plastic wrap and add the finishing touches to the jaws. I like to cut a chamfer on all edges using a drawknife, rasp, and spokeshave. The chamfer not only adds visual interest to the piece, it also makes the vise more user-friendly.

CARE AND MAINTENANCE

The beauty of a wooden saw vise is its ability to be maintained. Like a wooden handplane, a wooden saw vise can be tuned and repaired as atmospheric conditions and wear dictate.

If the top of the jaws get beat up over time, you can remove the leather by applying heat or moisture to the hide glue, then plane the top of the jaws smooth and glue a new strip of wood on top. After blending the new piece in with the existing jaw, glue the leather back on and get back to sharpening.

You can replace the jaw faces the same way, reintroducing new spring joints as you do.

A few coats of boiled linseed oil followed by a 50/50 blend of beeswax and paraffin are my go-to finish for shop tools. I use a polissoir to apply the wax and burnish the wood. The Acme screw will benefit as well from the same wax mixture—a few dabs on the threads will keep them operating smoothly.

USING THE SAW VISE

The longer front leg on the saw vise allows it to be secured several ways to your benchtop—it can be gripped in a face vise or leg vise. If you have an apron around your bench, a couple of dog holes and holdfasts can hold it in place.

The additional contact area created by the longer leg helps stabilize the vise during use.

Once the vise is securely mounted, slip in a saw, carefully adjust the tooth-line, clamp down on the wing nut, and get to sharpening.

With a proper saw vise such as this one, keeping your saws sharp is easier than ever before.

Classic joinery. A ⅝" dowel is used to drawbore the joint. I used an offset of approximately 1/32"; hardwoods don't require a lot. Using the ⅝"-diameter dowel greatly reduces the odds of it splitting while being hammered home.

Plastic fantastic. Using plastic wrap is a great way to hold the leather strips in place where traditional clamps won't work. The angles on the jaw make any normal clamping setup difficult. Because a lot of pressure isn't needed for this application, plastic wrap is ideal.

Make it safe. The 90° corners on the oak jaws can be sharp and dangerous. Adding a chamfer is made easier by securing the leg to your benchtop, allowing the jaw to overhang. This gives you access for easy shaping.

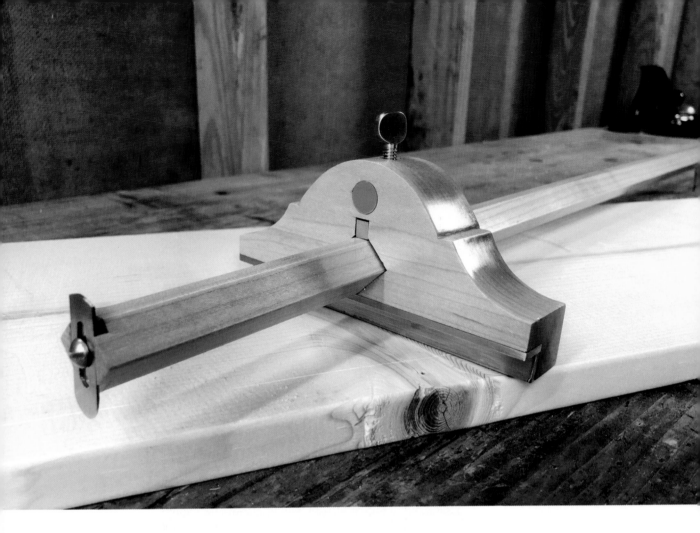

MAKE A WOOD & BRASS PANEL GAUGE

Learn how to work with brass and make an indispensable tool for hand work.

BY BOB ROZAIESKI

f you rip your stock on a table saw, your uses for a panel gauge are limited. If you make your rip cuts with a bandsaw or handsaw, however, a panel gauge is an indispensable tool. Its usefulness really shines when you need to mark out multiple wide panels to the same width, such as the sides of a carcase or the shelves of a bookcase. You can use a ruler and straightedge to perform this task, but the panel gauge is more efficient and precise.

PANEL GAUGE REQUIREMENTS

I built a simple panel gauge years ago. But after years of use, my old, poorly designed gauge is starting to get a bit worn and loose, affecting its precision and usability. I considered buying a new one, but there are few commercial options available and each has at least one shortcoming that I wasn't willing to accept. So I decided to build one.

My new panel gauge needed to meet several requirements. First, the beam

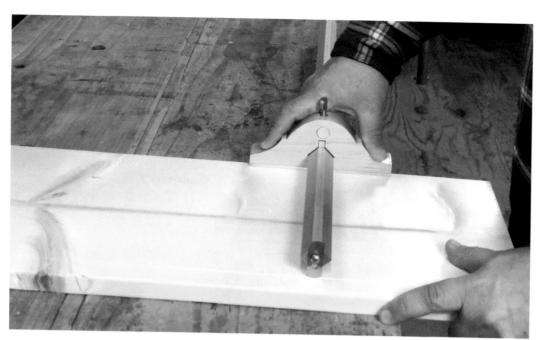

A less-common marking tool. While the panel gauge hasn't been common in most shops for more than 100 years, once you use one, you'll wonder how you ever managed without.

should be at least 28" long to allow marking out case sides up to 24" deep. Second, the beam must lock in place rigidly with no movement whatsoever. Third, the fence has to register solidly on the stock. Finally, the gauge must be able to mark both rough-sawn and milled lumber, which means it has to accommodate both a knife and a pencil.

This panel gauge also incorporates brass for the locking mechanisms and wear parts. Brass can be cut easily with a hacksaw and shaped with files. Tapping brass is also straightforward. Plus, it polishes it up nicely.

START WITH THE FENCE

I'm using 1¼"-thick hard maple for my gauge because it's a dense wood that will be resistant to wear, yet it can still be worked easily enough with hand tools. However, any heavy, dense hardwood will work just fine.

Mill the stock for the fence to dimension, then bore the holes for the beam mortise and ½" brass nut. The beam is pentagon-shaped, so that will lock down without any wiggle at all. In order

A valuable power tool. While I do 99% of my woodworking with hand tools, a bench top drill press comes in handy from time to time.

to lay out the mortise for this shape, start with a diamond by drawing lines tangential to the hole at 45° to the bottom of the fence.

After laying out the ¾" diamond mortise, chop the sides with a ¾" chisel. Work half way through the stock from either side, meeting your cuts in the center. The resulting mortise should be as clean and straight as possible so that the fence slides easily on the beam without being loose and sloppy.

Start with a diamond. The mortise for the five-sided beam starts out as a diamond shape, which is easily laid out with a combination square.

From diamond to pentagon. The top of the mortise is cut square to make room for the brass foot that will lock the five-sided beam in position.

Create a custom nut. Drilling and tapping a piece of round brass rod creates a simple, decorative captured nut for the thumbscrew.

After chopping the diamond, lay out the ¼" square mortise for the brass pressure foot on each face of the fence. To do this, measure ⅛" above and below the top point of the diamond (the center of the mortise) and draw lines parallel to the bottom of the fence. Similarly, measure ⅛" left and right of the top point of the diamond and draw lines perpendicular to the bottom of the fence. Chop out this mortise to a depth of approximately ⅛".

This will leave you with a section in the center that is still V shaped. Pare away the V-shaped material just to the tip of the diamond. You will end up with a mortise that is ⅛" deep x ¼" wide x ¼"high on each face, connected by a mortise that is about 1" deep through the center and ¼" wide x ⅛" high.

COMPLETE THE BRASS WORK

The nut for the thumbscrew is made from a short section of ½" round brass rod. In order to ensure that the hole in the wooden fence stock lines up with the hole in the ½" round brass nut, bore through both at the same time. Use a bit sized for the thumbscrew you are using (mine is ¼"-20).

Bore straight through the brass all the way into the beam mortise (a

CUT LIST & MATERIALS

NO.	ITEM	DIMENSIONS (INCHES)			MATERIAL
		T	W	L	
☐ 1	Fence	1¼	2¾	6	Hard maple
☐ 1	Beam	¾	¾	28	Hard maple
☐ 1	Nut	½-dia.	-		Brass rod
☐ 1	thumbscrew	¼-20	-		
☐ 2	Wear strips	⅛	½	6	Brass
☐ 1	Pressure foot	¼	¼	1½	Brass
☐ 1	Knife holder	⅛	½	1⅛	Brass
☐ 1	Card scraper				Knife

File the foot. While this piece looks difficult to make, it is actually quite simple. The inside faces don't need to look pretty—everything but the outer faces will be hidden when the gauge is assembled.

The finished foot. When the foot and beam are assembled into the fence, the foot will be captured in the U-shaped mortise above the beam.

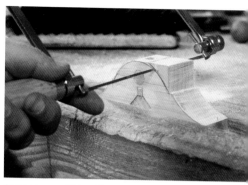

Shape to your liking. Once all of the brass is filed flush, the profile of the fence can be cut with a coping saw and shaped with files and scrapers.

drill press makes this step easy). Then, remove the ½" round brass stock and bore the hole in the fence larger to create clearance for the thumbscrew. Tap the hole in the ½" round brass stock to match the threads of your thumbscrew, and cut the brass stock slightly oversized with a hacksaw.

Make a ½" x ½" rabbet in the bottom corner of the fence to provide better registration of the fence on the stock being marked. Since the rabbet is subject to significant wear, attach a pair of ⅛" thick x ½" wide brass strips with 30-minute epoxy. These wear strips will help to lengthen the life of the fence. Leave them slightly oversized for now.

While you have the epoxy mixed, glue in the brass nut if you'd like (this step is optional but makes the gauge more user-friendly). To do so, insert it most of the way into the hole and add a bit of epoxy to the two ends before setting it all the way in. This will keep epoxy out of the threads. Make sure to get the thumbscrew hole aligned and the thumbscrew functioning before the epoxy sets up.

Now turn your attention to the pressure foot. This small brass foot is cut and filed to shape from a ¼" x ¼" x 1½" piece of bar stock and applies pressure to the top of the beam to lock it in place. Without this piece, the thumbscrew

would damage the top surface of the wood beam.

Once the epoxy has cured, all of the brass can be filed flush with the faces of the wooden fence. To hold the pressure foot in place for filing, wedge a small piece of soft pine in the beam mortise.

MAKE THE BEAM

The beam starts out as a ¾" square piece of maple. Plane the corners off the beam, leaving a small flat. To create the larger flat surface for the pressure foot to contact, plane the top corner down until the flat is about ¼" wide.

Bore a hole to fit a pencil about ¾" from one end. Make a vertical saw kerf through the end of the beam, through the center of the hole and about ¾" past the hole. In front of the pencil hole, bore a horizontal clearance hole for a wood screw on one side of the kerf, and a pilot hole on the other side of the kerf. By putting a wood screw in this hole, you can pull the kerf closed to clamp a pencil in the beam.

FIT THE KNIFE

On the opposite end of the beam, chisel a ½" wide x 3⁄16" deep notch. Cut a piece of the ⅛" x ½" brass stock and fit it to the notch. Bore and tap a hole in the center

Joiners saddles. Blocks with a V shape cut into them are useful for working on the corners of square stock.

Another brass nut. Another tapped piece of brass is the perfect way to attach a removable scribing knife.

Homemade scribing knife. A piece of an old handsaw or card scraper makes a simple scribing knife that is easy to sharpen with a file. A chainsaw file easily turns a couple of drilled holes into a slot.

of the brass for a #10-32 machine screw. Bore a shallow relief hole in the beam behind the brass so that the screw does not press into the wooden beam, and then epoxy the tapped brass strip into the notch. Once the epoxy has cured, file the brass flush with the beam.

You have several options for the knife. The easiest is to purchase a panel gauge knife. If you go this route, you may need to alter the size of the mortise at the end of the beam to fit the knife.

I made a knife from an old card scraper. To do so, cut a ½"-wide strip from the edge of the scraper. I used an abrasive cutoff wheel in a rotary tool. You could also clamp the scraper stock between two scraps of wood and use a hacksaw to cut through the wood and scraper at the same time.

File the cut edge until the blade fits into the notch in the end of the beam. Grind a curved cutting edge and bevel on one end of the knife. Drill a series of holes down the center that will become a slot for the mounting screw. Use a chainsaw file to connect the holes and smooth out the slot. Cut the knife to length, file the edges to remove the sharp corners, and polish the faces on a honing stone. You can then hone or file the bevel.

FINISH IS OPTIONAL

I go back and forth when it comes to finishing tools. On the one hand, applying a couple of thin coats of finish will protect the tool from dirt and keep it looking pretty longer. On the other hand, any film finish is going to wear away with regular use. For this gauge, I applied a couple of coats of an oil/varnish blend, lightly sanding with 600-grit sandpaper between coats. I don't know how long the finish will last. But I have no doubt that this new gauge will last me at least the rest of my lifetime.

SIDE VIEW

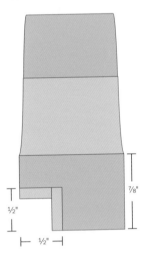

7/8"

½"

½"

FRONT VIEW

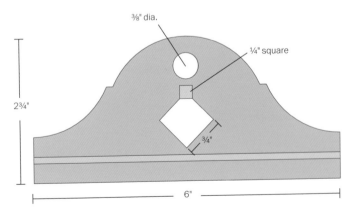

3/8" dia.

¼" square

2¾"

¾"

6"

HANDMADE SAW CABINET

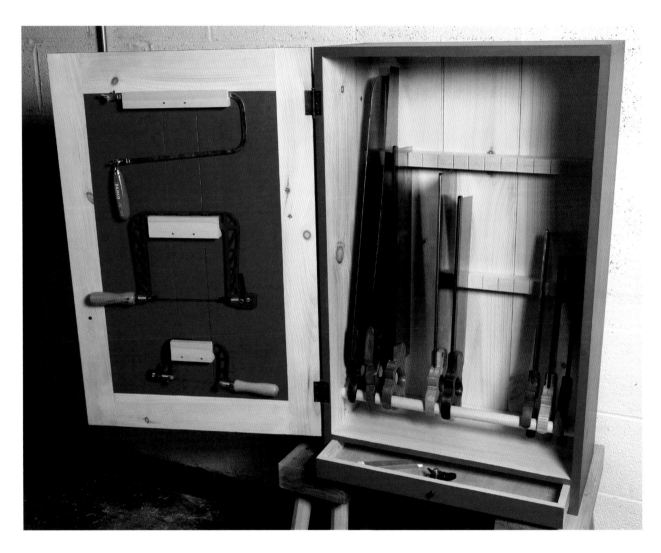

Use vital hand-tool techniques to build storage for your saw collection.

BY KIERAN BINNIE

Gazing into my tool chest and realizing my saw till was bursting at the seams, I had to face a sobering fact: I was in the grip of a backsaw addiction. I had two choices. Either I could trim my collection down to the regulation-issue three backsaws—dovetail, carcase, and tenon—or I could build a wall-mounted saw cabinet to hold my full collection.

This project was the result of choosing option number two. The bonus? Building the cabinet provided the opportunity to use many of my saws, with an emphasis on dovetail, dado, and mortise-and-tenon joinery.

MATERIALS AND DESIGN

I built my saw cabinet out of what is sold in the UK as Canadian yellow pine

Rabbets by hand. A rabbet or moving fillister plane makes quick work of the rabbets for the casework.

Saw guide. For a first-class saw cut, pare a channel into your knife line to guide the saw.

Light pressure. Gently resting your fingers on the back of the saw keeps it from jumping out of the cut.

(*Pinus strobus*, aka Eastern White Pine) as it is lightweight, strong, and dimensionally stable. Other similar softwoods would be appropriate, and hardwoods would also be fine, although you may want to beef up the French cleats to account for the extra weight of a hardwood cabinet. The kerfed blocks that capture the sawplates are hard maple to provide wear resistance, while the rail on which the saw totes rest is a length of 1" hardwood dowel of the sort most timber yards and big box stores sell. You could, of course, turn your own rail if you have a lathe and want some extra practice. See the cut list for the components.

This design will accommodate 14 saws, including full-sized 28" handsaws; if you want to store a 30" miter saw, increase the length of the sides. Saw totes can vary in size, and while the rail holds all of my saws so that they do not rest on the partition below, you might want to start by laying your saws on a full-sized drawing to make sure that your particular saws will not bottom out on the partition.

JOINERY

The casework is joined by through-dovetails at each corner. There are a number of steps before you are ready to dovetail. First, plane a ½" wide, ¼" deep rabbet on the rear edge of the sides and ends to accept the tongue and groove backboards. Next, lay out the dado for the partition separating the drawer from the main body of the till. The dado is ½" wide, ¼" deep, and situated 2 ¾" from the bottom edge of the carcase sides.

There are several ways to cut dados, and here is how I do it. Lay out the sides of the dado with a sharp marking knife. Deepen the knife line with a wide chisel (I use a 2" butt chisel) and then pare into the chisel line from the waste side, to provide a V-shaped groove deep enough for the set of your saw to be below the surface of the workpiece. This groove will guide your saw and is known as a first-class saw cut. Cut the walls of the dado with a fine crosscut saw, gently resting fingers of your off-hand on the toe of the saw to keep it in the cut. Chisel out the majority of the waste and clean up the bottom of the dado with a small router plane, working from both ends to the middle.

Finally, drill a 1"-diameter mortise in the sides to accept the rail on which the saw totes will rest. This mortise is 6" from the bottom, and 3" in from the front edge of the cabinet. Clamp both sides together and drill through them at the same time to ensure that the mortise lines up.

Because I cut my dovetail tails first, I also planed a shallow (1⁄16" deep) rabbet on each end of the tail boards. The dovetails are standard through-dovetails; I used six tails per side, and the tails are on the sides of the casework while the pins are on the ends. The only unusual feature is that the pin at the rear corner is a captured half-pin to account for the rabbet, so lay out a separate baseline for the half-pin. I gang-cut the tailboards and then lay out the pins for each corner.

With the dovetails cut, assemble and glue the four sides together, including the rail. Leave the rail over-length at this stage and allow the excess to protrude through the mortises. Once the glue has cured, fit and glue the partition, making sure the partition is flush to the rabbet at the rear of the casework. Let the glue fixing the partition cure, and then clean up the exterior of the casework with a smoothing plane.

BACKBOARDS

The three backboards are joined with tongue and grooves, and are held in place with a combination of cut nails

Drill reference. A small bevel helps to sight the angle the pilot hole for the cut nails on the backboards.

Production work. Gang-cutting the tails makes for efficient dovetailing. Cutting the same side of each tail helps keep a consistent angle, before cutting the opposite side of all of the tails. The captured half-pin hides the rabbet on the rear edge of the casework.

and glue. They should be a friction fit into the carcase, so take your time getting them snug. I started with fitting the two outer boards, and then adjusted the middle board to fit the remaining space. Tongue-and-groove both edges of the middle board, as well as the inner edge of the boards going on each side. A no. 49 plane makes quick work of the tongue and groove.

Once the panels are tongue-and-grooved and fitting nicely, glue just the long edges of the two outer boards into the rabbets on the case sides. Then nail the boards to the top and bottom of the case and to the rear edge of the partition. I used great-looking 4d wrought-head nails with excellent holding strength. The nails securing the ends of the boards need to be angled slightly so that they pass through the boards and into the ends of the casework; a small bevel is useful for sighting the angle while drilling the pilot hole.

DOOR

The door is standard frame and panel construction. The rails have a 2"-long

tenon on each end to fit into the stiles, and a 2"-deep mortise to accept the tenon of the middle stile. Start with the rails and the two outer stiles. Plough a ½"-deep, ¼"-wide groove on the inner edge of the four frame components, and then set a mortise gauge to the same spacing—leave this marking gauge set as you will need it for the middle stile and for the panels. The tenons are 2½" wide and have a haunch on the outer edge, sized to fit the groove ploughed on the stile. Use the marking gauge you just set to lay out the tenons on the rails, and then cut the tenons. I use the same

first-class saw cut method described above to guarantee clean tenon shoulders and a good gap-free fit.

Chop the mortises on the stiles (they should be 2 ½" deep and ¼" wide) and assemble the four frame components to check for square. I find it helpful to lay the frame on top of the carcase at this point to make sure everything is the right size.

Next up is the middle stile. Use a bar gauge to work out the length of the middle stile and allow for a 2½"-long tenon on each end. Plough a ¼" x ½" groove on both of the long edges of this piece and

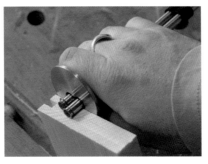

In the groove. Lay out the tenons with a marking gauge set to the dimensions of the groove.

Haunched tenon. The layout of the tenon—note the haunch on the right hand side.

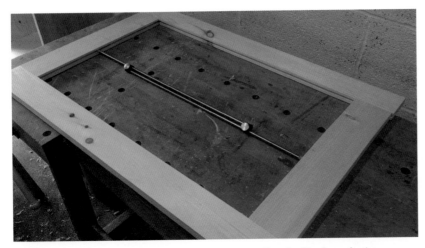

Make middle stile to fit. A bar gauge measures the internal length of the frame for the middle stile.

lay out the tenon using the same marking gauge settings as you did for the tenons on the rails. The only difference is that there is no haunch on the tenons of the middle stile. Layout the mortises on the rails so that the middle stile bisects the frame into two equal sections. With all the joinery cut, assemble the frame to check for square and measure the spaces for the raised panels (don't follow the cut list for this part of the build—your frame might be a slightly different size than mine).

The raised panels fit into the grooves of the frame on all four sides with a ¼"-thick, ½"-wide tongue. The tongue should be laid out so that the backs of the panels are flush to the back of the

frame. This will allow you to hang frame saws on the inside of the door. Use the same marking gauge as for the tenons and mortises to mark out the tongue. The front face of the tongue is created by raising the panels. I used a panel raising plane for this, although in a pinch you could use a jack plane. Once the panel has been raised to the edge of the tongue, flip the panel over and cut the second side of the tongue using a moving fillister plane. A ¼"-wide groove cut into a piece of scrap is useful for telling you when the tongue fits, and it is best to err on a slightly loose fit rather than being too tight.

When you come to assemble the door for the final time, glue both rails into

one stile, then slide in the first panel. Glue the tenons of the middle stile into the rails, and then slide in the second panel before fitting the final stile. The panels float in their grooves to allow for seasonal movement, so make sure that only the tenons and mortises are glued.

DRAWER

The shallow drawer is big enough to hold a set of saw files, as well as the file holder. Because I planned to milk-paint the saw cabinet, and because this is a piece for the workshop, I used through-dovetails for all corners of the drawer. You could use half-blind dovetails for the front, or even a simple nailed drawer; when it comes to workshop furniture, it is all down to preference and the time available for the build. Use the cut list as a guide, but be sure to fit the components to the cabinet on your bench rather than following the numbers slavishly. If you decide to dovetail the drawer, then placing the tails on the sides will reduce racking when pushing and pulling the drawer in use.

INTERNAL FITTINGS

The internal fittings are all simple to make. Start with the kerfed blocks that hold the sawplates. There are two blocks—one extending the full width of the cabinet for handsaws and large backsaws, with a shorter block half

Do it by hand. Raise the panels.

Sample mullet. A mullet the same size as your groove will tell you when the tongue is the correct width.

CUT LIST & MATERIALS

NO.	ITEM	T	W	L
			DIMENSIONS (INCHES)	
CASEWORK				
☐ 2	Sides	¾	11½	37¾
☐ 2	Ends	¾	11½	24
☐ 1	Partition	½	11	23
☐ 3	Backboards	½	8*	37¾*
☐ 1	Rail	1-dia.	-	25
☐ 4	Cleats	1	3	24
DRAWER				
☐ 2	Sides	½	2*	11*
☐ 2	Front and back	½	2*	22½*
☐ 4	Bottom	¼	10½*	1

NO.	ITEM	T	W	L
			DIMENSIONS (INCHES)	
DOOR				
☐ 2	Rails	¾	3½	22
☐ 3	Stiles	¾	3	35
☐ 2	Panels	¾	8¼*	29*
INTERNAL FITTINGS				
☐ 1	Backsaw kerfed block	1¼	1¾	22½
☐ 1	Handsaw kerfed block	1¼	1¾	15
☐ **	Frame saw hangers	½	2	**
SUPPLIES				
☐ 1	Oval knob			
☐ 1	Desk interior knob			
☐ 1	Solid brass butt hinge with ball tips			

* Fit to carcase
** Number of frame saw hangers and necessary length depends on frame saw collection

the width of the cabinet for smaller backsaws. Depending on the nature of your saw collection you may want to adjust the lengths of these blocks. Lay out the kerfs for the saw holders on 1¼" centers with a pair of dividers and mark their 1¼" depth on the sides of the blocks.

To make the kerfs, I used a miter saw mounted in a miter box—this ensures

neat kerfs that will be wide enough to fit most backsaws. If you don't have a miter box, then a crosscut backsaw will suffice. Test the fit of your saws and use a crosscut filed handsaw to widen slots as necessary. Use a chisel to cut a chamfer on each edge of the kerf—this will guide the sawplates into their resting place when you put saws in the completed cabinet. Drill pilot holes through the

rear of the blocks, making sure that the screws are spaced between the kerfs, and through the backboards of the cabinet. I used 1¼" no.8 screws to hold the blocks in place. Four evenly spaced screws is enough for the short block, and I used six for the full-width block.

Frame saws take up a disproportionate amount of space in my tool chest, so I decided to mount them on the inside of the door of the saw cabinet. Each hanging bracket is made of two pieces of ½"-thick, 2"-wide stock. Glue the two pieces together so that they overlap by ¾". Once the glue has cured, plane one side flush so that the bracket is an L-shape, and cut the bracket to length based on the size of your frame saw. It is easier to glue and work the brackets when they are larger pieces, so I made two large brackets, one of which I cut down to provide hangers for my two smaller frame saws. The brackets are then fixed to the inside of the door with 2d headless cut brads.

Brackets for the frame saws. These simple tool holders are fast to make and work surprisingly well.

Quick kerf. A miter box makes quick work of kerfing the saw holder.

FRONT PROFILE

Dovetailed corners

¾"

9"

24"

1¼"

10"

37¾"

12½"

1" rail

½"

3" center of rail to top of dado

2"

¼"-deep dado

SIDE PROFILE

11½"

Half-pin

Dovetails

¼"-deep ½"-wide rabbet

37¾"

1" rail

3"

6½"

BACK PROFILE

24"

* 8" * *

Tongue-and-groove boards (*reduce width to fit carcase)

37¾"

¼"-deep ½"-wide rabbet on all 4 sides

CABINET DOOR

24"

3½"

3"

3"

3"

7¼"

28"

35"

3½"

18"
(plus 4" for tenon)

2"-long 2½"-wide tenon

Cut nails. You can see the three rows of cut nails securing the backboards and the brass screws holding the kerfed blocks.

FINISHING UP

Before applying any finish, cut the mortises for the butt hinges and drill holes for the door and drawer pulls. Once you have fitted the hinges, remove all the hardware and apply your finish of choice. I used five coats of green milk paint, applied with a foam brush. Finally, I installed two French cleats on the cabinet to prepare for hanging the cabinet in my shop.

MORE THOUGHTS ON HOW TO STORE HANDSAWS

SHOULD I DRILL A HOLE IN MY SAW TO HANG IT?
BY GRAHAM BLACKBURN

In the shop I usually hang my saws by the handle over a peg or dowel. In my tool chest I store them on the underside of the lid by sliding the end of the blade into a slotted sleeve fixed to the under-side of the lid. Some woodworkers also drop the handle over a piece cut to match the hand hole (also fixed to the underside of the lid), which is then secured by a turn block. Alternatively, saws may be stored lengthwise but upright in a narrow compartment fitted with a slotted piece at each end—saws are then alternated left to right and right to left with the blade end dropped into one slot and the handle end dropped into the slotted piece at the other end.

Slot in saw till protects blade

I also usually provide my saws with a blade guard: this can be as simple as a narrow piece of wood the length of the blade, which is kerfed down the middle to slip over the teeth.

It may stay in place either by friction or, as the kerf becomes wider over time, by being held onto the blade with a rubber band. Traditionally it would have been held to the blade by a leather thong at each end. (The nib often found at the narrow end of handsaw blades serves to capture the thong at that end. The curved cutout invariably found in the handle of saws captures the thong at the other end of the blade guard). As for boring a hole in the blade I doubt that it hurts (much), but I wouldn't bother; some saws are actually manufactured with a hang hole, but lacking such a hole you can always hang the saw by the handle.

A UNIQUE STORAGE RACK
DESIGN BY JEFF ISLER, WRITTEN BY PAUL ANTHONY

If your saw collection includes a variety of handles that protrude too far from the wall, this storage rack might do the trick. It's made from a section of 4 x 4 post. The slots intersect angled holes that contain textured foosballs, which lock the blade against the side of the slot. Inserting the saw from the bottom of the slot moves the foosball upwards, while gravity and friction hold the saw in place. To remove a saw, simply lift it up and out.

Cut a length of 4 x 4, spacing the saw slots 2½" apart. Carry the layout lines across the top and face of the block, marking the ³/₁₆" slots and the 1⅜" holes so they intersect with the holes angled at

about 20°. Cut the slots on the table saw and drill the holes using a drill press.

In each hole put a 34mm, textured foosball. Slot and attach a piece of fiberboard on top to keep sawdust out of the holes. The completed rack can now be screwed to the wall.

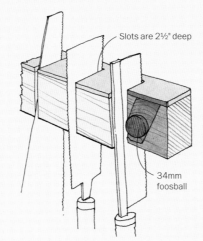

Slots are 2½" deep

34mm foosball

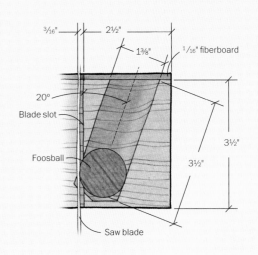

³/₁₆" | 2½"

1⅜"

¹/₁₆" fiberboard

20°

Blade slot

Foosball

3½"

3½"

Saw blade

SIX-BOARD CHEST

Put your saw skills to work with two planks, two days, and two piles of nails to make this classic piece.

BY CHRISTOPHER SCHWARZ

Six-board chests have been an enduring form of furniture in Western cultures for hundreds of years. And while they differ in their details during different ages, the basic form and the way it is built has been unchanged since the form appeared.

The chest here has details I've seen on chests in the 18th and 19th centuries. You can choose different moldings (or omit them), or add carving or a stenciled design to make the chest suit the time period you prefer.

DESIGN WITH THE BOARDS

I built my chest using an 8'-long board and a 12'-long board. Both pine boards were 18½" wide. If you don't have access to wide lumber, feel free to glue up panels to the final width. If your chest is painted, no one will notice.

Because my boards were 18½" wide, I used that fact to help design the chest—there's no need to rip 1" off a wide board or glue on 1". The design of these chests is pretty flexible.

I crosscut the 45"-long lid piece from the 8'-long board and set it aside. Why 45"? These chests are typically 32" to 48" long, and 45" was the clearest length of wood I could get from the board. This piece sets the length and depth of the chest.

With the lid cut, I cut the two ends, which determine the height of the chest. These chests typically range from 18" to 27" tall—a good height for a chest when it comes to lifting the lid and

Rip, then crosscut. If you rip the molding piece first before crosscutting the front from the back, you will get a nice long piece of straight-grained stock.

Twice as accurate. Ripping the long notches in the ends is easier if you sandwich the two pieces together. Your cut is more likely to remain square.

bending over to get something out of storage. It's not too high and not too low.

I cut the ends to 21" long from the remainder of my 8'-long board. This length allowed me to cut around some knots and eliminate some checks on the end of the board. I then set the two ends aside and grabbed my second board.

From this board I cut my front, back, bottom, molding, and battens.

When you cut molding by hand, the best way to do it is to "stick" one long piece of molding and then cut your three pieces from that piece. Sticking three pieces of molding is tricky; it's unlikely that you will be able to create

A plane job. Most of the clean-up of the notches is with a plane. Work to your layout lines and then clean up any excess in the corner.

Variations on a form. The blue chest is the one I built for this article—but let your wood and aesthetics dictate your build. (The yellow chest is by Timothy Henriksen; the green chest is by Ty Black.)

Around the bend. I lay out my ogee on both outside faces of the ends. This helps me make an accurate saw cut because I can peer over the board during the cut to ensure I'm on track.

The hungry chisel. A chisel takes a bigger bite than a router plane, so do as much work as possible with the chisel.

exactly the same molding profile on all three pieces.

Find a piece for the molding that is long enough to wrap around the front and two ends. (Molding on the rear of a chest is unnecessary.) Cut that piece free from your board, then cut the front and back pieces to size. The hard part is done. The remaining stock will be your bottom and lid battens.

JOINERY ON THE ENDS

The first step in creating the joinery for this chest is to deal with the end pieces. They have long notches cut into their long edges to receive the front and back. Not all chests had these notches, but they give you a cleaner look—the outside surfaces of the front, back and ends are all flush, even at the feet. They also make assembling the chest easier.

Some woodworkers create this notch by scabbing on a small bit at the floor. It seems like a good idea, but I don't have evidence that this was done on historical chests. Perhaps they didn't do it that way because these chests sat on dirt floors that got wet, and a hide glue joint there would come loose.

Cutting these long notches is easy. Sandwich the boards together and lay out the long notches—each is ⅝" wide and is as long as the front and back pieces are wide.

Pinch the sandwiched boards in your vise and saw the long notches. With the boards still pinched together, use a plane plus a chisel or rasp to true up the notch.

The last task while the ends are sandwiched together is to cut the decorative profile on the bottom of the ends that creates the feet of the chest.

The simplest profile is what antique dealers call the "bootjack"—it's a simple inverted V that resembles the tool used for pulling your boots off your feet. This profile is just two lines. A fancier profile is a half-circle or an ogee. Both of these

are laid out with a compass, cut with a frame saw, and smoothed with a rasp.

IN THE HOUSE

The next decision is whether or not to plow dados—housed joints—in the ends that will grasp the bottom board. Here are some pros and cons.

Pros: A dado lets you slide the bottom board in without any battens or glue blocks for support. You don't even need to add glue when sliding the bottom in place.

Cons: Cutting these dados requires extra tools and time.

I always opt for cutting the dados because it makes assembly easier. The first time you cut a long dado, you can nail or clamp a fence to your work to guide your saw. After a dado or two you will realize that the stiffness of the saw's plate is enough to keep you straight.

Saw the walls of your dados, then remove most of the waste with a chisel driven by a mallet. Finish the job with a router plane. The dado is ¼" deep, ⅞" wide, and begins 5" from the bottom of the end pieces.

FRONT AND BACK

The front and back pieces are a blank canvas—both for decoration and for joinery. Shallow (¼") rabbets on their ends help make the chest easier to assemble. And you can carve the front, which is typical of 17th-century chests. Or make some simple scratched decoration. Or grain paint it, which was typical in the 19th century.

Let's talk about the joinery first. The reasons to cut the rabbets on the front and back are simple:

1. Help preventing the case from racking after assembly—especially when transporting the chest.

2. Ease of assembling the chest alone. The rabbets lock into the notches in the end pieces; add a few nails.

EXPLODED VIEW

Width of rabbet on ends of front/back
= thickness of ends

Bottom fits in dados in ends.
Width of bottom = width between
notches in ends. Length of bottom
= distance between dado bottoms
when ends are in place with back

43¼"

16"

21"

18"

7⁄8"

Ends are ½" narrower than
top. Top is width of widest
board available

Length of notch = width of
front/back. Depth of notch
= thickness of front/back
beyond rabbet

Length of front and
back = length of top
less the thickness of
both battens

3. You can get away with using shorter (and cheaper) nails. If you make this chest using 1"-thick stock, you need 8d nails to assemble the carcase. However, if you cut ¼"-deep rabbets in the front and back pieces, you can use 6d nails instead. If you buy handmade nails, the savings add up.

Cut your ¼"-deep rabbets with a simple rabbet plane or a moving fillister plane. If you are using a simple rabbet plane, first knife a line where you want the shoulder of the rabbet to be. Tilt the plane and put a corner of the tool's sole into the knife line to turn the knife line into a V-shaped trench. Then continue to plane until you complete the rabbet. You'll need to tip the plane a little off vertical at first. Then you'll need to tip it vertical.

Cut the rabbets. They don't need to be deep—¼" is perfect—but they need to be consistent in depth so that your carcase is square and everything is flush on the outside. Make the rabbets 7⁄8" wide to match the thickness of your ends.

With the rabbets complete, clean up the inside surfaces of your ends and the

WHY SIX-BOARD CHESTS SURVIVE

When you examine these chests as a builder, they are a bit of a puzzle. The puzzle isn't how they go together, but instead, how they stay that way over time.

These chests disobey many rules of wood movement. The grain on the front and back of the chest is horizontal. The grain on the ends is vertical. The front and back should have split and fallen off. And take a gander at the lid. The grain of the battens that help keep the lid flat and the dust out is 90° to the grain on the lid.

By all rights, the battens should have fallen off, the lid should have split and the whole chest should be a collection of interesting splinters.

Nails—the right nails—allow you to get away with serious crimes of wood movement. Nails are almost always more flexible than screws or dowels. So a nail allows the wood to expand and contract, bending back and forth through the yearly humidity cycles.

Except for hardened masonry nails, I've found that all nails will bend, including wrought nails, cut nails, wire nails, and pneumatic ones. The reason I've always preferred cut nails for making furniture is that they hold better than wire or pneumatic nails. Cut nails are a wedge that—when properly driven—bend and crush the wood fibers in a way that holds the nail fast.

Wire and pneumatic nails aren't wedges, and while they do compress some of the surrounding wood fibers, they are just not in the same league as cut nails (or wrought nails).

Another bonus: A good cut nail will have a rough finish, especially compared to a smooth wire nail. That rough finish also gives the nail some extra bite. This is why many pneumatic nails are coated with a glue that helps them stick in the wood—every little bit helps.

Squaring rabbets. Cross-grain rabbets help square the carcase and line up the pieces during assembly.

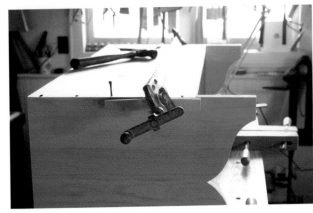

Head in. Cut nails with a broad head are the ideal fastener for attaching the front and back to the ends. You can use nails with a smaller head for attaching the bottom.

front and back. This is the best time to do this because you are about to nail some things together.

NAIL THE BACK TO THE ENDS

If you've cut rabbets and dados in your parts, here's how to assemble the chest: Nail on the back (add glue if you like). Fit the bottom in the dados. Nail on the front. Then nail the bottom in place.

But first, there are some details to consider. The length of your nails should suit the amount of wood that wasn't rabbeted away in the front and the back boards. If you have 1"-thick stock and cut a ¼" rabbet, then you should use 6d nails—8d if you're working in pine. If you have ⅞"-thick stock and cut a ¼"-deep rabbet, you can use 5d nails—6d in pine.

You need a nail with a sizable head for this operation—such as a rosehead. Headless nails or plain brads won't do

because they don't have enough holding power. Depending on your stock, you might need to drill a pilot. In some pines and with some nails, you won't. So make a test joint in scrap to find out what holds and what doesn't split. After some experience you will get a feel about what will work.

One last detail: Angle these nails at a small slope—about 5°. Alternate the slopes with every nail. This slope helps keep the front and back wedged onto the ends.

With the back nailed to the ends, cut the bottom board to slide into the dados so the fit is snug and the carcase is square. This is a hand-tool way of approaching the bottom: Create the opening and fit the piece to the opening. If you are machining your bottom, you should be able to hit the length bang-on and nail the bottom onto the ends first.

Usually when I make the bottom with hand tools, it ends up too thick for the dados. Instead of reducing the thickness of the entire bottom, I bevel the underside of the ends—like a raised panel—until the bottom slides in.

I glue the bottom in place all around—then nail it in after assembly. The glue helps here because all the expansion and contraction is in your favor. So take advantage of it.

You don't need to use fancy nails to secure the bottom. Just use 6d or 8d cut finish brads—four through each end and five or six through the front and back. Set these below the surface if they will be covered by molding.

STICKING IT TO THE MOLDING

Skip the molding if you are going for a plain chest. But the molding adds the appearance of a classic plinth—the visual separation between the base section and the not-base section. Surviving pieces were made both ways—with and without molding.

Cut the molding on an 80"-long piece of stock. Then cut the miters. This ensures that your profiles will match at the miters. I profile the molding on a sticking board—a long and flat board with a high fence. I used a ⅜"-square ovolo for this profile.

ON MITERING

The less you fuss about mitering, the better your miters will be. Just cut them with confidence and calm. I wish someone had told me that when I was starting out.

Wrapping molding around three sides of a carcase is cake compared to making the full 360°. Focus on getting one corner good and tight. Then clamp those two pieces in place on the chest and mark the other corner for its miter.

With both miters cut on the front piece you can focus on getting the fit tight on the returns (the pieces that

CUT LIST & MATERIALS

NO.	ITEM	DIMENSIONS (INCHES)			MATERIAL	COMMENTS
		T	W	L		
☐ 1	Lid	⅞	18½	45	Pine	
☐ 2	Ends	⅞	18	21	Pine	
☐ 2	Front and back	⅞	16	43¼	Pine	¼" rabbet both ends
☐ 1	Bottom	⅞	16¾	42	Pine	In dados in ends
☐ 2	Battens	⅞	⅞	18½	Pine	

Miter slices. Here is how you miter your stuck molding. By sawing close to your line you can make the grain and profile match around the corner perfectly.

Bent over. Clenching the nails back into the molding hooks the battens to the underside of the lid.

for the screws so the lid can move. The other approach is to drive nails through the battens and the lid so that the tips protrude through the molding, then bend the tips back into the molding.

Choose nails that protrude about ½" beyond the molding. Then turn the tip of the nail over like a fishhook and drive it back into the molding. This secures the batten to the lid and keeps the lid fairly flat.

HINGE AND FINISH

There are a variety of ways to attach the hinges to the carcase and lid. Snipe hinges are an old solution (you can make your own using 2" cotter pins).

These chests were typically painted on the outside and left bare inside. The paint highlights the form of the chest and obscures the distracting cross-grain aspects of the form.

What paint you choose should be based on:

■ Do you hate strong smells? Use latex.

■ Does the paint need to be bomb-proof? Consider oil-based.

■ Do you want a traditional look? Use commercial milk paint.

■ Are you a glutton for punishment? Make your own paint.

I use commercial milk paint. I know it's not historically accurate, but it does give me a look I like. Plus it is quite durable and fairly low on the toxicity scale. I apply two coats of paint and sand between the coats with a 320-grit sanding sponge.

After building several of these chests, both by myself and with friends, I found that the process became faster and faster (two days is almost a luxurious amount of time). In fact, it took longer to type this explanation of building the piece than to actually make it.

"return" down the ends of your chest). I leave the returns long until after everything is glued and nailed in place.

Glue the entire front of the molding to the case. On the returns, glue only the miters and the front one-third of the molding to the ends. Press everything in place for a minute or two. Then drive the brads. The molding should not shift. Set the brads. Then saw the returns flush at the back of the carcase.

ABOUT THE LID

The lid has two important components: its molding profile around the rim and the battens on its underside. The molding profile makes the lid look like something more sophisticated than leftover siding. The battens keep the lid flat—if you attach them correctly.

First cut the molding profile on the two ends and the front of the lid. It can be almost any profile you have on hand. I have a larger ovolo plane (½" wide) that looks like a lot of other lids for chests that I've seen. Cut the profile on the ends first, then on the front edge. This allows you to erase any splintering from working across the grain.

The battens on the ends of the lid keep it flat. Nailing the battens to the lid isn't enough—the battens will fall off when the top moves. Gluing the battens won't do. Nailing and gluing is better, but the lid's movement is still stronger than that joint.

You have two choices: old school and modern. The modern approach is to screw the battens to the underside of the lid and ream out the pilot holes

CONTRIBUTORS

MANUFACTURERS

TOOLS AND SUPPLIES

Visit your local woodworking store or look online for these brands mentioned in the book.

Augusta-Heckenrose (Western saws) en.augusta-heckenrose.de

Blackburn Tools (saw filing guide) www.blackburntools.com

E. Garlick & Son (Western saws) www.flinn-garlick-saws.co.uk

General Finishes (milk paint) generalfinishes.com

Gramercy Tools (bow saw; saw vise) toolsforworkingwood.com

Horton Brasses (knobs; hinges) www.horton-brasses.com

Independence Tool (dovetail saw) www.lie-nielsen.com

Japan Woodworker (Japanese saws) www.woodcraft.com

JapaneseTools.com (Japanese saws, Nano Hone)

Knew Concepts (coping saw) www.knewconcepts.com

Lynx (Western saws) www.flinn-garlick-saws.co.uk

Marc Adams Woodworking School **www.marcadams.com**

McMaster-Carr (Acme handle nuts) www.mcmaster.com

Olsen (coping saw; coping saw blades) www.olsonsaw.net

Paragon (Western saws) www.paragon-supply.com

Pax (Western saws) www.flinn-garlick-saws.co.uk

Pegas (coping saw blades) www.scies.ch

Sandvik/Bahco (Western saws) www.bahco.com

Stanley (open-frame miter box) www.stanleytools.com

Starrett (saws; hand tools) www.starrett.com

SuperTool.com (hand tools)

Tandy Leather Supply (leather) tandyleather.com

Veritas (saw filing guide) www.veritastools.com

VintageSaws.com (sharpening tools; sharpening service; restored handsaws)

VINTAGE AND RETIRED BRANDS

If you can find one of these brands at an auction, antique store, or yard sale, it may be worth your while to pick up an old quality tool.

Adria (joinery saws)

Augusta-Heckenrose (Western saws)

Crary Machine Works (coping saw)

Disston (handsaws)

E.C. Atkins (handsaws, coping saw)

E. Garlick & Son (Western saws)

Enco (Acme threaded rod and nuts)

Independence Tool (dovetail saw)

Lynx (Western saws)

Millers Falls (fully framed miter box)

Pax (Western saws)

Simonds (handsaws)

Spear & Jackson (handsaws)

Tashiro Hardware (ZETA saws)

Wenzloff & Sons (Western handsaws)

Wheeler, Madden & Clemson (handsaws)

Woodjoy Tools (bow saw)

INDEX

Note: Page numbers in *italics* indicate projects/accessories. Page numbers in parentheses indicate intermittent references.

Publisher: Paul McGahren
Editorial Director: Kerri Grzybicki
Design & Layout: Clare Finney
Indexer: Jay Kreider

Cedar Lane Press
PO Box 5424
Lancaster, PA 17606-5424

Paperback ISBN: 978-1-950934-63-8
ePub ISBN: 978-1-950934-64-5

Library of Congress Control Number: 2021938264

Printed in the United States of America
10 9 8 7 6 5 4 3 2 1

Note: The following list contains names used in *The Essential Handsaw Book* that may be registered with the United States Copyright Office:

Adria; Augusta-Heckenrose; Blackburn Tools; Crary Machine Works; Disston; E.C. Atkins; E. Garlick & Son; Enco; General Finishes; Gramercy Tools; Highland Woodworking; Horton Brasses; Independence Tool; Japan Woodworker; JapaneseTools.com; Knew Concepts; Lee Valley Tools; Lie-Nielsen Toolworks; Lynx; Marc Adams Woodworking School; McMaster-Carr; Millers Falls; Olsen; Paragon; Pax; Pegas; Sandvik/Bahco; Simonds; Spear & Jackson; Stanley; Starrett; SuperTool.com; Tandy Leather Supply; Tashiro Hardware; Tools for Working Wood; Veritas; VintageSaws.com; Wenzloff & Sons; Wheeler, Madden & Clemson; Woodcraft Supply Corp; Woodjoy Tools.

To learn more about Cedar Lane Press books, or to find a retailer near you, email Info@CedarLanePress.com or visit us at www.CedarLanePress.com.

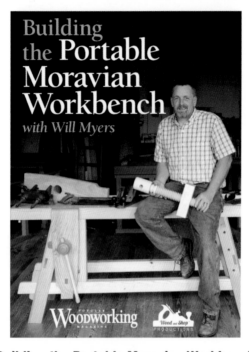
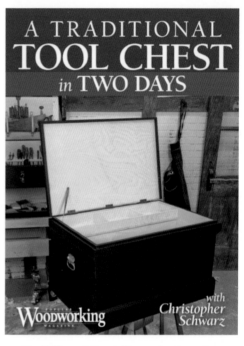

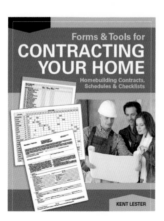
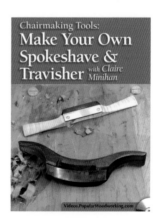

DISCOVER THE APPEAL OF A TRUSTY HANDSAW

Ask most woodworkers about their introduction to handsaws and a memory of a rusty blade stuttering and sticking its way through a cut comes to mind. Throw in terms like "fleam" and "rake" and a handsaw's place in a world of power tools seems even more antiquated and mysterious. This is too bad, because a properly sharpened and correctly used handsaw can become one of the most efficient and trusted tools in any workshop.

With expert know-how compiled from the pages of *Popular Woodworking*, *The Essential Handsaw Book* will change your perception and introduce you to everything you need to know to master handsaws, backsaws, and specialty saws. You'll learn correct sawing techniques, the sharpening process, and how to hand-cut dovetails. After upgrading your knowledge and abilities, you can apply your newly honed skills to creating sawbenches, a bench hook, a classic six-board chest, and more. With the tips, tricks, and information of *The Essential Handsaw Book*, you'll soon understand the efficiency and ageless appeal of a properly used handsaw.

978-1-950934-63-8 $24.95 US

CEDAR LANE PRESS
www.cedarlanepress.com

52495 >
9 781950 934638

HIP TO BE SQUARE

20 CONTEMPORARY CROCHET DESIGNS USING 5 SIMPLE SQUARES

KATIE JONES

Crochet Designer Katie Jones, alongside her mum Annie, runs a brand that's purpose is to show you how to make fun, colourful, hand crocheted pieces, embracing the sustainable practices of an old craft while giving it a new twist. Upon graduating from Central Saint Martins in 2013, Katie's designs have since been stocked in luxury stores and featured on the pages of fashion and craft publications worldwide. Her Granny Square creations have been showcased at The Victoria and Albert Museum as part of its Fashioned from Nature exhibition and in the window of Selfridges' Oxford Street Store as part of their Bright New Things Award. Her work now focuses on championing the Make-It-Yourself revolution, showing you how to consciously craft your own amazing pieces!

@KATIEJONESKNIT